(abinet

55 Washington St, # 327
Brooklyn NY 11201 USA
tel + 1 718 222 8434
fax + 1 718 222 3700
email info@cabinetmagazine.org
www.cabinetmagazine.org

Summer 2006, issue 22

Editor-in-chief Sina Najafi
Senior editor Jeffrey Kastner
Editors Jennifer Liese, Christopher Turner
UK editor Brian Dillon
Associate editors Sasha Archibald, Ryo Manabe
Art director Brian McMullen
Graphic designer Leah Beeferman
Assistant editor Courtney Stephens
Editors-at-large Saul Anton, Naomi Ben-Shahar, Mats Bigert, Brian Conley,
Christoph Cox, Jesse Lerner, Frances Richard, Daniel Rosenberg, David Serlin,
Debra Singer, Margaret Sundell, Allen S. Weiss, Eyal Weizman, Margaret
Wertheim, Gregory Williams, Jay Worthington
Website directors Luke Murphy, Kristofer Widholm
Contributing editors Joe Amrhein, Molly Bleiden, Eric Bunge, Pip Day, Charles
Green, Carl Michael von Hausswolff, Srdjan Jovanovic Weiss, Dejan Krsic, Roxana
Marcoci, Phillip Scher, Lytle Shaw, Cecilia Sjöholm, Sven-Olov Wallenstein
Editorial assistants Ned Kihn, Michelle Legro, Kavior Moon, Maggie Murphy,
Eric Nylund
Cabinet National Librarian Matthew Passmore
Prepress Zvi Lanz @ Digital Ink
Founding editors Brian Conley & Sina Najafi

Printed in Belgium by the rock-solid men and women at Die Keure

Cabinet (USPS # 020-348, ISSN 1531-1430) is a quarterly magazine published
by Immaterial Incorporated, 181 Wyckoff Street, Brooklyn, NY 11217.
Periodicals Postage paid at Brooklyn, NY and additional mailing offices.

Postmaster:
Please send address changes to Cabinet, 181 Wyckoff Street, Brooklyn, NY 11217.

Individual subscriptions
1 year (4 issues): US $28, Canada $34, Western Europe $36, Other $50
2 years (8 issues): US $52, Canada $64, Western Europe $68, Other $95

Subscriptions address: 181 Wyckoff Street, Brooklyn, NY 11217
Please either send a check in US dollars made out to "Cabinet," or mail,
fax, or email us your Visa/MC/AmEx/Discover information. Subscriptions
also available online at www.cabinetmagazine.org or through Paypal
(paypal@cabinetmagazine.org). For back issues, see the last page of this issue.

Institutional subscriptions
Institutions can subscribe through EBSCO or Swets, or through our website.

Advertising
Email advertising@cabinetmagazine.org or call + 1 718 222 8434.

Distribution
Email circulation@cabinetmagazine.org or call + 1 718 222 8434.

Cabinet is available in the US and Canada through Indy Press Newsstand Services,
which distributes via Ingram, IPD, Tower, Armadillo News, Small Changes, Last
Gasp, Emma Marian, Cowley, Kent News, Media Solutions, The News Group,
Newsways, Primary Sources, Total Circulation, Ubiquity, Newbury Comics, Disticor,
and Don Olson Distribution. If you'd like to use one of these distributors, call
+ 1 415 445 0230 ext 114, fax + 1 415 445 0237, or email maire@indypress.org.

Cabinet is available in Europe and elsewhere through Central Books, London.
Email: orders@centralbooks.com

Cabinet is available worldwide as a book (with ISBN) through D.A.P./
Distributed Art Publishers. Tel: + 1 212 627 1999, Email: dap@dapinc.com

Submissions
See www.cabinetmagazine.org or email submissions@cabinetmagazine.org.

Cabinet is a non-profit 501 (c) (
Contributions to Cabinet are fu
such contributions; please con
Donations of $25 or more will
Donations above $100 will be
made out to "Cabinet." Please

Cabinet wishes to thank the fo
their support of our activities c
to the extraordinary contribution of the Flora Family Foundation from 1999 to
2004; without their generous support, this publication would not exist. We would
also like to acknowledge David Walentas/Two Trees for their generous donation of
an office in DUMBO, Brooklyn. All contact information remains unchanged.

$100,000
The Annenberg Foundation

$30,000
The National Endowment for the Arts

$15,000
The Greenwall Foundation

$10,000 – $14,999
The New York State Council on the Arts
Stina & Herant Katchadourian

$5,000 – $9,999
Helen & Peter Bing

$2,500
Nick Debs

$1,000 or under
Hesu Coue & Edward Wilson, Barbara & Richard Debs, Tim Patridge, Debra Singer
& Jay Worthington

$500 or under
Monroe Denton, Sheila Lambert, Julia Meltzer, Nancy Spero (in memory of Leon
Golub), Owen Walton

$250 or under
Elizabeth & Chris Apgar, Jennifer Bacon & Filippo Fossati, Elizabeth Casale,
Laura & Fred Clarke, Molly Davies, E. V. Day, Michael Duffy, Charlotte & Bill
Ford, Evan Gaffney, Joy Garnett & Bill Jones, Josh Harlan, Craig Konyk, Jason
Middlebrook & Kate Needham, Richard & Lenore Niles, Jason Olin, Cay-Sophie
Rabinowitz & Christian Rattemeyer, Magda Sawon & Tomas Banovich, Michelle
Snyder, Susan Swenson & Joe Amrhein

$100 or under
James Bristol, Robert Everett-Green, Kathleen Gill, Frederick Loomis, Dana Maisel,
Alessandro Palmeri, Siri von Reis, Yael & Jacob Schori, Adnan Selimovic, James
Simmons, Alexis Turner

Erratum: We regret that the captions in Brian Dillon's article "Fragments from a
History of Ruin" in Cabinet no. 20 failed to credit Michel Makarius's book *Ruins*
as the source of the images accompanying that article.

Cover: Hasse Persson, *Say Cheese, Larry*, 1980. At the time this photograph was
taken, Larry Hagman's character, J. R. Ewing, on the television series *Dallas* epito-
mized the sense of entitlement and cock-suredness that came to characterize
Reagan-era America. *Dallas*, more than any other show, symbolically brought an
end to the anxieties and insecurities that had been the hallmark of 1970s America.

Page 4: A trichobezoar, or hairball, successfully removed during surgery from
the stomach of a twelve-year-old girl in 1964. From age six she had suffered from
trichophagia, an emotional disorder causing a person – most often a girl entering
puberty – to eat their hair. Photo courtesy National Museum of Health & Medicine,
Armed Forces Institute of Pathology.

Back cover: Nina Katchadourian, *Small Barnacled Rock*, 2002.

COLUMNS

MAIN

INSECURITY

AND

CONTRIBUTORS

Alan Berger is Associate Professor of Landscape Architecture at Harvard University Graduate School of Design. He is author of the award-winning *Reclaiming the American West* (Princeton Architectural Press, 2002) and *Drosscape: Wasting Land in Urban America* (Princeton Architectural Press, 2006), books which use aerial photography and mapping to reveal waste in the American landscape.

Adam Broomberg and Oliver Chanarin are a photographic team based in London. They were the editors and principal photographers of *Colors* magazine and are the author of three photographic books. *Chicago*, their most recent book project, will be exhibited at the Steven Kasher Gallery, New York in October 2006. See <www.choppedliver.info>.

Andrea Codrington is a Brooklyn-based writer and editor specializing in design and architecture. She is currently at work on her first novel.

Maggie Cutler, the winner of *Cabinet*'s "editor-by-chance" lottery in issue 19, is a writer and editor at the satirical website <www.shacklereport.com>. Her articles appear in a wide assortment of publications.

Brian Dillon is UK editor of *Cabinet*, and writes regularly for *Frieze, Modern Painters,* and *Art Review*. His memoir *In the Dark Room* (Penguin) won the inaugural Irish Book Awards non-fiction prize, 2006. He is working on *Tormented Hope: Nine Hypochondriac Lives,* to be published in 2008.

Kate Ferencz is an artist who until recently lived in Providence.

Miklos Gaal is a Finnish photographer. He is represented by Hermann & Wagner Gallery, Berlin, and by Anhava Gallery, Helsinki.

Rubén Gallo is the author of *Mexican Modernity: The Avant-Garde and the Technological Revolution* (MIT Press, 2005) and *New Tendencies in Mexican Art: The 1990s* (Palgrave, 2004). He edited *The Mexico City Reader* (University of Wisconsin Press, 2004) and teaches literature and cultural studies at Princeton University.

Xavier Girard is a writer, curator, and teacher specializing in modern art and Mediterranean culture. He frequently writes on cuisine.

Joshua Glenn is a Boston-based writer and editor, currently for *The Boston Globe*. In the 1990s, he was editor and publisher of *Hermenaut*, a philosophy and pop culture journal.

Valentin Groebner has written on images of extreme violence (*Defaced: The Visual Culture of Violence in the Middle Ages*, Zone Books, 2005), and on gifts and corruption (*Liquids Assets, Dangerous Gifts*, University of Pennsylvania Press, 2002). He teaches medieval and Renaissance history at the University of Lucerne, Switzerland, and is currently working on the commodification of human bodies and body parts in Renaissance Europe and in the twenty-first century.

Jackie Dee Grom is an environmental consultant who currently resides in Chicago. In fall 2007, she will continue her graduate studies in Arctic and Subarctic geomorphology and permafrost hydrogeology associated with current global climate change at McGill University in Montreal.

Cathy Haynes is researching a Ph.D. at Goldsmiths College, London, on the limits of the animal and the human in Franz Kafka, Max Ernst, and Georges Bataille. She is also Head of Interaction at Artangel <www.artangel.org.uk>.

Benjamin Kafka is a member of the Princeton Society of Fellows. In 2007, he will become an assistant professor in the Department of Culture and Communication at New York University. He is completing a book entitled *The Demon of Writing: Paperwork and the Making of Modern France*.

Jeffrey Kastner is a New York-based writer and senior editor of *Cabinet*.

Nina Katchadourian is a Brooklyn-based artist. She is represented by Sara Meltzer Gallery, New York and Catharine Clark Gallery, San Francisco.

Michelle Lopez is an artist based in New York City. For more information, visit <www.michellelopez.com>. Her current curatorial effort, "Exit Music (For a Film)," will open at Grimm/Rosenfeld Gallery, New York, on 27 January 2007.

Brian McMullen is art director of *Cabinet* and a regular contributor to *The Believer*. This summer, he will join *Bomb* magazine as managing editor.

Gage McWeeny is an assistant professor in the English department at Williams College. He is currently at work on a book about sociality and antisociality in Victorian literature called *The Comfort of Strangers*.

David Miles is an artist who lives and worries in Brighton, England. He has shown his work in Europe, North America, and South America. For more information visit <www.davidmiles.info>.

Eileen Myles lives in San Diego and New York, where *Hell* – an opera for which she wrote the libretto – was produced at P.S. 122 in April 2006. She is currently finishing up a novel, *The Inferno*, about the hell of being a female poet.

Sina Najafi is editor-in-chief of *Cabinet*.

Shimon Naveh is a retired brigadier general in the Israel Defense Forces and director of its Operational Theory Research Institute.

Reviel Netz is Professor at Stanford University, with appointments in the departments of Classics, History and Philosophy of Science and Technology, Philosophy, and History. His many publications range widely, from the history of human cognition to poetry in his native language, Hebrew. His co-authored book (with William Noel), *The Archimedes Codex: Uncovering the Secrets of Archimedes ' Palimpsest,* is forthcoming next year from Weidenfeld & Nicolson.

James Oles writes mainly on modern Mexican art. He splits his time between Mexico City and Wellesley College, where he teaches in the Art Department and is adjunct curator of Latin American art at the Davis Museum and Cultural Center.

Sally O'Reilly is a London-based writer, lecturer, and producer of performance-based events.

James Peel is a graduate of the Royal College of Art. He is a multimedia conceptual artist who has exhibited at Tate Liverpool and the Henry Moore Institute and is currently a resident of the Emmanuel Hoffman Foundation in Basel, where he is working on a series of projects that explore the nature of rainbows and the music of waterfalls in relation to the forgotten universal language of Solresol, invented by Jean François Sudre in the mid-nineteenth century.

Hasse Persson is a photographer, writer, curator, and director of the Borås Museum of Modern Art in Sweden.

Sarah Pickering is a London-based photographer who received her M.A. in photography from the Royal College of Art in 2005. A recipient of the Photographers Gallery Graduate Award and the Jerwood Award, she has exhibited in the UK, Mexico, and the US – most recently with a solo show at Daniel Cooney Fine Art, New York. Her work will also be featured in *Vitamin Ph,* the forthcoming Phaidon anthology on contemporary photography.

Dorion Sagan is co-author of *Into the Cool: Energy Flow, Thermodynamics, and Life* (University of Chicago Press, 2005), a book which links all growth and complexity to the dispersal of energy described by the second law of thermodynamics.

Tal Schori currently lives and works as a freelance designer in Mexico City. Formerly the manager of Storefront for Art and Architecture, he will enter the Master of Architecture program at Yale this fall.

David Serlin is an associate professor of communication and science studies at the University of California, San Diego, and an editor-at-large for *Cabinet*. He is the author of *Replaceable You: Engineering the Body in Postwar America* (University of Chicago Press, 2004).

Jenny Tobias is a librarian at the Museum of Modern Art, New York, and a student in the Ph.D. Program in Art History at the Graduate Center of the City University of New York.

Eyal Weizman is an architect and director of the Centre for Research Architecture at Goldsmiths College, London.

Christine Wertheim teaches writing, literature, and feminism at the California Institute of the Arts, where she also organizes an annual conference on contemporary writing experiments. She is the co-director of the Institute For Figuring.

Gaby Wood is a New York-based author and a staff writer at the *Observer*, London. A version of her essay in this issue was originally published in *The Phantom Museum* (Profile Books, 2003).

THING / NO. 3

Given *Cabinet*'s sprawling network of correspondents around the world, and given that that world is so thick with "things," we expected to be inundated with submissions to this, our occasional column known as "Thing." As it happens, there has been a rather perplexing dearth of suitable entries—one series of cryptic Polaroids, received over the course of several weeks in the summer of 2004 and depicting a smallish pink plastic tarpaulin draped over an unidentified object in a variety of settings, nearly made the cut, though it was ultimately adjudged by the committee that they depicted the covering of a thing rather than the thing itself, and thus were disqualified. With all this, readers will understand our great excitement in discovering the enigmatic little doo-dad pictured below at actual size. As always, we've passed it on to an expert panel for their learned assessment.

Several medical equipment shops line the narrow road leading to the UNAM Medical School in Mexico City. I pass these businesses frequently on my way to the Copilco Metro station, and have become particularly fond of the veterinary lab supply store. A ragtag assortment of photocopies cover every inch of the shop's front window. These copies excerpt key information from the literature that accompanies each item available within, and are tagged with circular, fluorescent stickers indicating each item's inventory number in ballpoint pen. Seen from the street, the display resembles a gigantic, polka-dotted bulletin board.

Recently, the excerpt for Item #172 caught my eye. Unusually, this one supplied an image—a photograph of a man in business attire awkwardly struggling to insert a cotton swab into the rectum of an anything but compliant stork. Hoping to discover additional photos in the complete text, I entered and asked the veterinary student behind the counter about Item #172. She retrieved a hermetically sealed, sterilized, plastic package containing two items. The first was a cotton swab, and the second is the receptacle we see here. The literature I sought was taped securely to the back of the package in a tightly folded square, so I purchased the item, which cost about two bucks.

The results were rather disappointing. The information sheet included no additional photographs, instead presenting detailed diagrams relating to the proper collection of avian fecal matter. I had purchased a kit to collect such matter for testing for the deadly H5N1 strain of avian influenza. The swab is used to collect the fecal matter. It is then inserted through the top (white) portion of the receptacle, breaking a thin plastic seal that ensures the receptacle's sterility prior to the swab's introduction. Once the swab is fully inserted into the primary cavity of the receptacle, the white lever is depressed, simultaneously sealing the receptacle and releasing a saline preservative solution from the ancillary "bunny-ear" cavity to ensure that the sample does not dehydrate, which would render H5N1 undetectable.

The back of the sheet introduces Dr. Richard Hyun, the subject of the photo. An independent ornithologist, Dr. Hyun founded the Hong Kong-based Friends of At-Risk Oriental Storks (FAROS) in 1999. In the panic over a possible human pandemic of bird flu, the Oriental Stork (*Ciconia boyciana*), among other endangered migratory bird species, has been slain in a misguided attempt to curb the spread of the disease. Since 2003, FAROS has expanded its mission beyond the Oriental Stork and has proven instrumental in providing various institutions with these sampling kits to encourage testing, to ensure appropriate collection methods, and, most importantly, to avoid the indiscriminate slaughter of healthy birds. The pamphlet closes with the (hopefully) immortal words of Dr. Hyun, "We must remember that this is a War on Bird Flu, not a War on Birds."

— Tal Schori

I found Favrace one October evening standing outside my apartment door. I may never have noticed him had I not dropped my keys by accident. Small and blue and apparently shy, Favrace stood quite still, as if he wished me away. It was only after asking him a second time whether I could help him that he responded.

"Just waiting," he said, and it sounded like a flugelhorn blowing into a goose-down pillow. It was the first and last time I ever heard Favrace say anything.

When I opened the front door, he moved inside and settled into the bedroom, although for the life of me I don't remember him having feet. After eating and taking a bath, I dozed in front of the TV's blue stutter. Favrace made soft whirring noises in the corner, which I took as a sign of contentment.

I soon found out that Favrace was very particular. He liked seltzer, Chet Baker, Vicks VapoRub, and scabs. He hated flannel, anything having to do with eggs, direct sunlight, and cooking shows.

One day, I came upon the idea of leaving the Food Network on for Favrace during the daytime, since nothing bad ever seems to happen in televised kitchens. It turned out to be absolutely the wrong thing to do. From then on, any time I watched *Iron Chef*, Favrace would hide under the chair in an agitated state. His white bits—I'm uncertain of the proper anatomical terminology—would pump up and down and soon the room would smell of lemons and tears. I thought about opening the windows to air out the apartment, but I became concerned that Favrace might do something drastic. I got rid of my TV instead. You can never be too careful.

Sometimes I brought dates home to meet Favrace, but this usually led to more smell combinations—occasionally pleasant, but more often than not foul. They were different for every person. P. provoked Victorian hospital carbolic, while T. got something vegetal and distinctly fermented.

"Oh Favrace," I'd say, leaning against the door after the date left. "What am I going to do with you?" That's usually when I would put on a Chet Baker album and he would jitter around the floor in obvious pleasure.

Without the distraction of TV or romance, I was able to spend more quality time with Favrace in the evenings and on the weekends. I even checked with the human resources department at my company about the possibility of working from home a few days a week.

Ironically, it was the day that my home office furniture arrived that Favrace went missing. I am not suspicious by nature, but I am almost sure that one of the deliverymen slipped him into a pocket while I was turned the other way. For weeks I had a hard time sleeping at night thinking of Favrace in the back of a moving van hurtling toward a Perth Amboy office complex or a Cherry Hill nursing home.

It's been six months now, and I'm sad to say that the flyers and letters to the local press have done little to locate Favrace. Still, the pain of his absence is starting to dull; sometimes I even feel optimistic that he will find his way back. Today, for example, I walked down the street and the trees, newly budded, smelled like sex and the color green. As if Favrace were wishing me a happy spring.

—Andrea Codrington

Forget *The Da Vinci Code*, that ham-fisted compendium of half-baked claptrap. You want psychedelic revelations about the artificial nature of reality? Want ringside seats for the never-ending battle between radical change agents and the oppressive forces of epistemological orthodoxy? Look no further than the 1968 animated movie *Yellow Submarine*, an *Argonautica*-meets-*Alice in Wonderland* musical fantasy in which the Beatles voyage across space and time to free a utopian Pepperland from the Albigensian Crusade-style depredations of the Blue Meanies. Need proof that the quest for gnosis is a threat to established institutions? Look no further than the object pictured here, in all its obscene materiality.

Directed by George Dunning and art-directed by Heinz Edelmann without any input from the Beatles themselves, *Yellow Submarine* was an exercise in misprision, a creative misreading of an influential text—in this case the 1967 album *Sgt. Pepper's Lonely Hearts Club Band*. The film's effort to construct a coherent narrative from *Sgt. Pepper's* was every bit as paranoid, really, as Charles Manson's near-simultaneous effort to do the same with the Beatles' so-called *White Album*. But *Yellow Submarine* was also paranoid in the they're-out-to-get-us sense because the film portrays the powers-that-be as always looking to crush gnosticism.

How, exactly, is *Yellow Submarine* a gnostic movie? It's obvious once you know what to look for. The gnostic attempt to achieve intuitive knowledge of the infinite is enacted by the yellow submarine's voyage out of the material world into Nowhere Land. Also, the gnostic desire to be united with one's higher self is perfectly articulated by the "John" figure, who, upon encountering the Lonely Hearts Club Band, sagely opines that they're "extensions of our own personalities suspended, as it were, in time, frozen in space." And the religio-political establishment's aggressive determination to be humanity's sole conduit to divine wisdom? It's expressed by the Chief Meanie's dictum: "Let us not forget that heaven is blue ... Tomorrow the world!"

Audiences at the time were shocked by Edelmann's employment of "limited animation," an inexpensive alternative to Disney-style cartoon realism in which cels and sequences of cels are animated on top of static cels. Yet limited animation, even if it did pave the way for Hanna-Barbera crappiness, is what Marshall McLuhan called a cool medium: Its low definition of information requires viewers to participate actively in the creation of meaning. Given the movie's gnostic message, this medium is only appropriate. "John," "Paul," "George," and "Ringo" (who aren't voiced by the actual Beatles), not to mention the Nowhere Man, the Chief Meanie, and the movie's other figures, aren't characters but symbols. And—as we've been instructed most recently by the paintings of Laylah Ali—in order to engage the imagination, symbols must remain flat abstractions. ("You surprise me, Ringo," says the John figure at one point in the film. "Dealing in abstracts.") Creative misreading, which is a good way of describing gnosticism in general, is impossible unless the 3-D "real world" is flattened out into symbols pregnant with discoverable and inventable meaning.

As for the object in question, it's a rare *Yellow Submarine* merchandising tie-in, a weapon referred to but never actually pictured in the movie: not the Meanies' Anti-Music Missile or the Dreadful Flying Glove but the O-blue-terator. It was doubtlessly conceived and produced by the pop-culture arm of the anti-gnosis institutional complex to which I have already alluded. It's obscene not merely because it's an epistemological WMD for kids, but because *Yellow Submarine* cannot and should not be three-dimensionalized.

—*Joshua Glenn*

INVENTORY / BELOVED
KATE FERENCZ

For this drawing, taken from a series called "Three Days For Trying To Care About Dead People I've Never Met," I read the *Providence Journal* obituaries, making note of whether or not each of the deceased was specifically described as being "beloved." Based on this criterion, I made drawings dividing the dead into "beloved" and "not necessarily beloved" categories. In each section, I re-drew the little portraits that had been printed in the newspaper; under each, I wrote the person's name and age. I tried to get accurate likenesses, treating everyone the same regardless of whether they were beloved or not.

I wanted to use the act of drawing these dead strangers as a way of spending time with them. It's counter-intuitive to be sincerely affected by the death of someone I never knew; these drawings are an attempt to organize, both on paper and in my mind, forces that are beyond my control or understanding. I can't really miss or love the people depicted in these drawings, but I wanted at least to make an effort to recognize their faces.

BELOVED:

CHERISHED:

Harold J. Harris
76

Rocco J. Fanello
54

Edward P. Bingaman
88

In Memoriams: people who must
have been cared about because someone
put an ad in the newspaper commemorating
thier death years afterward, specifically
mentioned as being loved and not

LOVED:

NOT SPECIFICALLY
AS BEING LOVE

NO PICTURE:
BEN AMALFITANO

Robert C. Lawlor

*Roslyn "Rose" A. Major   *

ber 30th 2005:
beloved and those who were not

NOT NECESSARILY BELOVED:

onald J. St. Jean
47

Sandra J. Piacente
57

Orlando Sinapi
84

*Albert E. Leal
54

Grace Bissonnette
91

William "Billy" Flori
62

NO PICTURE:
MICHAEL A. RICCI, 85
JOHN R. MARTELL, SR, 90
*DR. CAROL J. CARGILL
SANDRA J. (MALO) GULA, 62
*SYBIL BLISTEIN KERN, 81
*MARY MAGDALENE (PERRY) McCANN, 69
JUNE (YEAW) REIFF, 78
PAULINE CAISSE CAPPUCCILLI, 85
*RALPH H. LAKEY, 81
RONALD S. STRANG, 70
*JOAN N. SILVERSTEIN,

TIONED

Garry Vaslet * Freda C. Rohloff

> *marks people who we are given reason
> to believe were loved although it
> is not stated outright.

COLORS / TAWNY
EILEEN MYLES

I drove up to Santa Barbara this weekend with the question under my belt of whether CA is tawny or not. I thought this is something I can do while I'm driving. The driving is a new problem. I mean I love driving because it is the greatest opportunity to listen to music and music pretty much comes from young people with few exceptions so I'm sailing up the coast on someone's young vibes and a bright slap of marigold is zipping along the highway with me for a while but you know marigold is such a businesslike color. It's usually the one bright color an otherwise boring situation has to offer in the way of energy. It's like "bright." This is unrelated to tawny but I'm just letting you see how I open up the color. The biggest driving problem (and this has been true for a while, but before I lived in CA it was chiefly on book tours I had this problem) is that while aimlessly driving across America (my favorite thing in the world to be doing) I get stabbed by an idea—and maybe I have a big pad of paper next to me on the seat but usually I have some fucking receipt for gas (most likely) and a big thought comes—one like this:

When Moses hit the rock with a stick and water came he didn't think great now I can always do that.

Obviously I can't lose that thought nor the one about tawny so—do I write it down? I bought an iPod for this specific purpose—so I can connect an iTalk to it and then talk into it when I drive in my truck. But then it turns out you can't plug an iPod into my truck. I could if I had a cassette player but no, I have a CD player, which doesn't do the trick.

There's another radio way so I bought that product but San Diego has so many bandwidths all used up with you know wonderful conservative radio yapping. How much does Jesus love you. A big sign over the freeway says this. It's his back with his arms extended. He loves you this much. And the sun of course is pouring down his backside. Is Jesus tawny is a thought. Having failed utterly to record my thoughts by pressing a button while I drive I have instead devolved in another direction. I call myself. After Eileen delivers her cheery greeting I go: I drove up to Santa Barbara this weekend with the question under my belt of whether CA is tawny or not. Satisfied I hang up.

It's interesting: there's a wall along the freeway over there and there's green dabs of paint every so often on it and a sun pouncing down. It feels kind of warm so the color isn't right but there's a feel. I'm thinking tawny isn't a color. It's a feeling. Like butter, the air in Hawaii, a feeling of value. Is anyone tawny who you can have. You know what I mean. It seems a slightly disdained object of lust. Her tawny skin—face it, used that way it's a corrupt word. It isn't even on the speaker. It's on the spoken about. She or he is looking expensive and paid for. So I prefer to think about light. Open or closed. Closed is more literary light. Or light (there you go) of rooms you pass as you walk or drive by but most particularly I think as you ride by at night on a bike so you can smell the air out here and see the light in there, the light of a home you don't know and feel mildly excited about, the light you'll never know. Smokers with their backs to me standing in a sunset at the beach are closer to tawny than me.

In Santa Barbara I hooked up with Bruce and Jill and before we parted we went to such a restaurant, awful by the sea. One of Jill's friends was in a wheelchair looking out at the sea and I just thought how rough for him to be in this place looking out and imagined the landscape of tawny being huge for him. Unbridled, the whole world. I don't think of disabled as being less but tawny is even more somebody else's if you never go to the beach alone anymore and there you are looking out. I don't smoke and so I think of Bruce as having more access to tawny than me standing there on the horizon having a smoke being nostalgic because there's little else to do when you're smoking pretending to feel. I miss it. I miss it exactly like that. The cigarette being a little rouged by light.

Jill and I talk quickly about pussy while Bruce is away. Getting any. You slept with Chris. Two hundred hours. That's all anyone got. That's amazing. Chris was this very cute butch who died of cancer a few years ago. My age. And I'm not stone like Chris but I'm a bit of a man, and yet before she died she wanted to give *me* a massage. And that was a feeling. Her kind dying hands rubbing all over my body. I gave myself up to whatever feeling she had, and it was in the late afternoon and the grass in her backyard was spectacularly green. The feeling was golden. Have I said it. Pretty much yes. It's a beautiful sadness.

Driving back down the coast the next afternoon (spent the night in LA) after deciding tawny was not what CA had it's more of an East Coast word I had it all alone in the late afternoon driving. I want to return to Moses for a moment. He probably thought this will never happen again. He looked around. What can I possibly say.

opposite: Michelle Lopez, *Car*, 1998. Child's convertible driving vehicle covered in vegetable-tanned leather. Courtesy the artist.

INGESTION / THE SOUP OF THE DEAD
XAVIER GIRARD

All night long a huge cloud of dead wood and green mud poured into the bay like milk boiling over. It is so cold that our teeth chatter as we laugh. We run through the rain in muddied streets, searching for a thick winter *pesto* that burns the tongue. As we open the door of the restaurant *Acchiardo*, located in the shadows of the *jesuiti*, in a haze redolent of daube, ravioli, and dark wine, the *mangiafagioli* hardly raise an eyebrow. The obituary of the day includes "soup of the dead." The owner brings it to us in heavy white plates. It's a soup *in brodo* (in bouillon) of great simplicity: water slightly colored with a few chickpeas, the remains of some pig's feet—such as Rabelais ate in his spelt soup at La Devinière—and two sage leaves. "There's nothing simpler," explains Acchiardo: "You soak three hundred grams of dried chickpeas for twelve hours, you cook them over a low flame in a good liter of salted and peppered water for three hours. After three-quarters of an hour, you add three hundred grams of sliced pork breast—I use pancetta, which is tastier—a clove-studded onion, and several pig's feet in pieces. Seven minutes before the end of the cooking, you add the sage leaves, then serve it boiling hot in a hollow plate like these, sprinkled with a trickle of olive oil, and there it is! The soup of the dead."

We close our eyes. My friend Jean-Paul Marcheschi, whom I brought here, lowers his head towards the plate and inhales with all his being, like the worshippers of the ortolan, an invisible vault over his head. "During my childhood," he murmurs, "near Cap Corse, not far from Pedre Scritte, on the night of the 1st to the 2nd of November, we ate this with *tiani* (Soissons beans) and *salviata*, that serpentine bread kneaded with wine and flecked with sage. This was the stone soup, the poorest of soups, an archaic dish originating in pagan times. We called it 'eating the heads of the dead.' The soup of oracles! *La mummia*—a substance resembling dried cod made from Egyptian mummies and sold at the price of gold between Sfax and Marseilles—had the same divinatory virtues. It comforted the dead during their journey. In order not to offend them, it was forbidden to speak or to blow. We gulped it down in silence, trying not to sniffle. When we finished, the bones of the pig's feet were scattered over the bottom of the plate, like remains after the pillage of a tomb." The plate steams gently upon the checkered tablecloth. We examine it like the walls of caves. The liquid is so clear that we could count the chickpeas and discern the island of pig's feet in the bronzed lake. "It's the isle of the dead," he tells me. "We drink the water of the Styx, the depth of a well of memory, directly from the manger of the shades."

A bit of grated *parmigiano reggiano*, almost powdery, very strong and acidic, and a dribble of green olive oil upon the emerging reliefs, and we plunge, like the diver of Paestum, into this soup of the abyss—with, as the saying goes, "the dead as our companions." The bouillon is peppery, yet a touch of very fine lard ends up sliding under the chickpeas, with their so tender and sugary flesh, to spread out into the greenness of the olive oil and the pungency of the parmesan. Little by little, we let ourselves be inhaled by its depths. We don't eat, we don't cut into our soup, we unearth our dead, we oscillate between two waters, amidst the nocturnal confines, joined together with the sea of omens. When we return to the surface, the bean-eaters look at us, mocking, as if we had dipped our spoons into the gruel of Hades.

Translated by Allen S. Weiss

This article first appeared in *La pensée de midi* No. 13 (2004), a special issue on "La cuisine, un gai savoir," edited by André Pitte, Xavier Girard, and Thierry Fabre.

opposite: Sage leaf gamely trying to cross the soup of the dead.
Photo Ryo Manabe & Eric Nylund.

MEXICAN RADIO GOES TO THE NORTH POLE
RUBÉN GALLO

When wireless broadcasting began in the 1920s, artists and writers around the world were gripped by what some historians have called "the madness of radio." A frenzy for the new technology seized enthusiasts from Paris to Mexico City and led to some outrageous tales: a Chicago doctor believed newborns could be educated by being wired to receivers, and a Mexican poet proposed designing miniature earphones for parrots in order to spare their owners the trouble of teaching them to talk. But of all the mad wireless projects from the 1920s, one stands out for its fantastic twists and turns: the story of El Buen Tono, Mexico's largest tobacco company, which in 1923 opened its own broadcasting station and launched a series of campaigns that would be more at home in a Futurist story by Velimir Khlebnikov than in the headquarters of a cigar manufacturer.[1]

El Buen Tono was owned by Ernest Pugibet, a French immigrant with a fetish for technology who was obsessed with linking his company to the most modern inventions. He already owned a blimp and a hot-air balloon that navigated the skies of Mexico City promoting the virtues of smoking Buen Tono cigarettes, and could not resist allying his company with one of the sexiest and most mysterious inventions of the modern era. Pugibet might have suspected that there was something incongruous about a tobacco company's decision to launch a radio station, so he decided

to make his project seem more logical by launching a new brand of cigarettes called "Radio." A photograph of El Buen Tono's stand at Mexico City's 1923 radio fair shows a proud Pugibet standing in front of an enormous radio receiver, surrounded by banners urging visitors to "Smoke 'Radio.'" To give visitors a taste of the future, the women who tended the booth wore radio antennas on their heads and carried baskets full of Radio cigarettes. And while their radio hats were not sophisticated enough to catch radio programs, the women-antennas were extremely successful at catching potential customers for El Buen Tono, at least if we are to judge from the crowds gathered at the company's stand.

El Buen Tono was not the only company hoping to capitalize on radio's desirability as a novel technology—in the same years, for example, Cervecería Moctezuma introduced a "radiophonic beer"—but El Buen Tono certainly outdid its competitors when it came to creative advertising. At one point, the tobacco company realized that not many Mexicans had radio receivers, so it decided to launch a new campaign focused on exchanging empty cigarette packs for radio parts: three for a pack of batteries; fourteen for a pair of earphones; twenty for a "Ritter set" receiver.

The most intriguing—and puzzling—advertisement was one for Radio cigarettes published in a literary journal called *El Universal Ilustrado*. The ad was similar to others in which

above: El Buen Tono's stand at the radio fair, Mexico City, June 1923. Courtesy SINAFO–Fototeca Nacional, Mexico City.

the company had urged consumers to "smoke Radio," but this time the caption appeared under a most unusual image: the pack of Radio cigarettes appeared over what looked like an iceberg, was crowned by a giant blimp, and flanked by a man wearing a fur coat and smoking a cigarette.

Fumen "RADIO"

El Mejor Ciga-rro por el Menor Precio

"EL BUEN TONO,"
S. A.

Who was this Nordic-looking man and why was he promoting El Buen Tono's cigarettes? Why would a Mexican tobacco company choose an icy landscape as the backdrop for a product that was grown in the tropics? And what was the connection between radio and the blimp, another invention of the modern era that fascinated Ernest Pugibet? Looking through newspapers from 1926—the year the ad was first published—I was able to uncover a tale that was even more bizarre and even more fantastic than the android cigarette sellers or the radiophonic beer. It turns out the advertisement had to do with a news item that was the talk of the town in Mexico City during the summer of 1926.

In the first days of May of that year, the Norwegian explorer Roald Amundsen, a seasoned adventurer who had been the first man to reach the South Pole, set out on an ambitious expedition to the North Pole. This time he did not board a ship or fly an airplane, as he had done in previous journeys, but settled for a means of transportation that was as implausible as his itinerary: an enormous zeppelin, almost 350 feet long, which he patriotically

called the *Norge*. Amundsen explained that a hydrogen-filled dirigible had many advantages over an airplane. "An airship," he wrote in an account of his expedition, "floats in the air even if all the motors should fail."

Amundsen's zeppelin, equipped with a large crew that included mechanics, radio telegraphists, and weather observers, departed from Spitsbergen in northern Norway, and embarked on a route that was to take it across the Polar Sea, over the North Pole ("the top of the world," as the explorer called it in his journals), and down the other side of the globe to Alaska. The logistics of the trip were extraordinarily complex: since there were no dirigible repair facilities in the Arctic, Amundsen took the precaution of shipping elaborate kits, composed of hundreds of spare parts, to every scheduled stop along his route. And to keep in touch with the world below, he had a powerful radio apparatus installed aboard the blimp, a floating station capable of sending and receiving meteorological forecasts, travel details, and a time signal.

Against all odds, Amundsen's journey was a success. He reached the North Pole on 12 May 1926 and immediately ran to the *Norge*'s Marconi room to send a radio telegram announcing the good news. The message, written in abbreviated, run-on language reminiscent of Marinetti's "words-in-freedom" and other avant-garde poetry, conveys the excitement felt by the explorer: "WHEN NORGE OVER NORTH POLE WAS GREATEST OF ALL EVENTS THIS FLIGHT," and even offers a brief but compelling description of the Polar landscape: "ICY WASTES WHOSE EDGES GLEAMED LIKE GOLD IN THE PALE SUNLIGHT BREAKING THROUGH FOG WHICH SURROUNDED US STOP."

When Amundsen landed safely in Alaska as scheduled, he instantly became a celebrity: reports about his journey were broadcast by radio around the world, and photographs of him appeared on the front pages of every major newspaper from Moscow to Buenos Aires. In Mexico City, accounts of the Norwegian's feat dominated the press during the summer of 1926. Photos of Amundsen and his zeppelin appeared almost daily in the city's most prominent publications, from *Revista de Revistas* to *El Universal Ilustrado*. *Excélsior*, the country's most important newspaper, serialized Amundsen's travel journal and proudly announced to its readers that the text had been sent wirelessly from the United States—where Amundsen was spending a few days before returning to Scandinavia—by "direct radiogram, exclusively for *Excélsior*."[2] The paper's New York correspondent even secured an exclusive interview with the explorer that appeared on the front page on 4 July 1926.

Part of the reason the Mexican press was so interested in Amundsen had to do with a freak incident of radio transmission: as the explorer reached the North Pole, he tuned his

above: El Buen Tono's advertisement for Radio cigarettes, *El Universal Ilustrado*, 8 July 1926.

opposite: The *Norge*. From *Air Pioneering in the Arctic: The Two Polar Flights of Roald Amundsen and Lincoln Ellsworth* (New York: National Americana Society, 1929).

onboard receiver and happened upon a program sent into the airwaves by El Buen Tono's station, which had recently acquired a powerful short-wave transmitter. The incident, reports radio historian Jorge Mejía Prieto, "became one of [the radio station's] greatest points of pride,"[3] and inspired the image of Amundsen on the North Pole, standing under his zeppelin and pointing to a box of Radio cigarettes and smoking. The ad copy—"Smoke 'Radio'"—urges readers to follow suit.

For El Buen Tono, the news about Amundsen's polar reception was a dream come true. As is clear from its ad campaigns, the company was out to modernize Mexico one citizen at a time, turning every smoker—and by extension every Mexican—into a radio listener fully attuned to the sounds of modernity. By smoking Radio and listening to our station, the ads seem to reason, every Mexican will become a modern subject. And could there be a more perfect model for this ideal than Roald Amundsen? The Norwegian was an archetypal modern man: he traveled in flying machines, crisscrossed the world with the ease of Hertzian waves, and he listened to the radio—not just to any radio, but to El Buen Tono's sparkling, modern short-wave broadcasts. The tobacco company hoped not only to turn every smoker into a radio listener, but every Mexican into an Amundsen.

Curiously, though most radio histories point to Amundsen's polar reception as one of the highlights of Mexican broadcasting, none of the historians provides more details

about the fantastic event. What exactly did Amundsen hear on the radio? How did he identify the source station? When did he contact El Buen Tono and what did he tell the station? Since the answers were nowhere to be found in the scant publications on the subject, in August 2004 I embarked on an expedition to the Mexico City archives determined to uncover the entire story.

My first stop was El Buen Tono's radio station, which is, surprisingly, still on the air and operating on the same frequency as in the 1920s, although it is no longer owned by the tobacco company. Once inside the offices, my inquiries about the North Pole broadcast were met with blank looks and a slight suspicion, not entirely unfounded, that I too was afflicted with the "madness of radio." No one there had ever heard about Amundsen, but the manager invited me to tell the Norwegian's strange story on the air instead.

My next stop was the newspaper archive at UNAM, the National University, where I scoured past issues of *Excélsior* in search of more details. This time I had better luck, and I was able to find the puzzle's missing pieces and correct the record on the explorer's Mexican connection. Amundsen, it turns out, did not really hear Mexican radio on the North Pole. What really happened was this:

In mid-June 1926, after the news of Amundsen's expedition had been featured on *Excélsior*'s front page almost every day for weeks, El Buen Tono seized the occasion to promote its cigarettes. The company launched a new ad for

Radio cigarettes showing Amundsen at the North Pole and announcing "Amudsen [sic] has said it: the true conquerors of the North Pole are El Buen Tono's 'Radio' cigarettes. El Buen Tono, the company of world-wide fame."[4] These were the days before truth in advertising, and a week later the cigar manufacturer launched an even more daring ad featuring the same image of Amundsen smoking on the North Pole: "The first thing Amundsen did as he flew over the North Pole was to smoke a 'Radio' cigarette: the cigarettes famous throughout the globe." The ever-cautious and safety-obsessed Norwegian explorer would have certainly been horrified at this scene of recklessness: a lit cigarette could have blown the *Norge* to a million pieces!

It appears that years later, when browsing through archival clippings, El Buen Tono's managers took the ad copy literally, and spread the word that the explorer had indeed said what the spreads claim him to have said. There was a curious slippage from smoking to listening, from cigarette consumption to radio tuning, and thus the image of Amundsen smoking Radio was read as proof that the explorer had listened to El Buen Tono's radio station. This misreading of Amundsen's polar reception eventually found its way into Mejía Prieto's *Historia de la radio y la televisión en México*, and his account was later repeated verbatim by other historians.

El Buen Tono's radio signal never reached the explorer, but the Radio campaign effectively brought Amundsen to Mexico. Though in real life the explorer never visited, the ad campaign transported him to Mexico, at least symbolically, since his name and photograph were delivered to every Mexican family that subscribed to *Excélsior*. In July 1926, the newspaper reported that a group of local enthusiasts had invited the Norwegian to visit Mexico and give a series of lectures about Arctic travel, but the explorer politely declined. He told a reporter that he was too exhausted from his polar trip and simply wanted to go back to Norway and get some rest. In any case, "the explorer," the newspaper concluded, "was very pleased to hear that he was well-known in Mexico, and he expressed gratitude for the praiseworthy reports of their deeds published in *Excélsior*."[5] Amundsen, it seems, was only drawn to icy corners of the planet—the Antarctic, the North Pole, Norway—and had little use for a tropical country like Mexico.

The explorer's Mexican fans were not discouraged by this lack of interest, and they continued to celebrate his prowess until after his death. When Amundsen lost his life in 1928—he vanished in the Arctic as he was flying to rescue a fellow explorer from a dirigible crash—two prestigious learned societies in Mexico City organized an elaborate homage to his life and deeds. The proceedings were published in a booklet titled *Sesión solemne en homenaje al ilustre explorador de los polos Roald Amundsen*. The meeting was attended by over one hundred Mexican scientists, and featured a keynote speech on Amundsen's explorations by Agustín Aragón, who extolled the Norwegian as a "model citizen," a "tireless lover of ice," and compared his heroic adventures to those of Don Quixote and

the Spanish *conquistadors*. "May Roald Amundsen rest in peace," one of the orators concluded, "and may History write his name in characters that will be remembered for all eternity for his virtuous and generous deeds."[6]

The story of Amundsen tuning in to Mexican radio over the North Pole turned out to be merely a clever advertising ploy devised by El Buen Tono, nothing more than a fantasy full of cigarette smoke and mirrors. But fantasies—as Freud demonstrated in his discussions of dreams, slips of the tongue, and other parapraxes—can tell us a great deal since they almost invariably represent "the fulfillment of a wish." It is easy to see what wish was being fulfilled in El Buen Tono's fantasy about its radio station: that Mexico, a country that during the Revolution had become increasingly isolated and cut off from the rest of the world, could finally take its place among the community of modern nations. The whole world was talking about Amundsen's feat, and the cigarette manufacturer's claims allowed Mexico—and El Buen Tono—to share center stage with the Norwegian explorer. During a time marked by great expectations, the company's radiophonic fantasy propelled Mexico, a poor country recovering from a devastating civil war, from the margins to the "top of the world."

1 For more on "the madness of radio," see the chapter titled "Radio" in my *Mexican Modernity: the Avant-Garde and the Technological Revolution* (Cambridge, Mass: MIT Press, 2005).

2 *Excélsior*, 6 June 1926, p. 1.

3 Jorge Mejía Prieto, *Historia de la radio y la televisión en México* (Mexico City: Octavio Colmenares Editor, 1972), p. 34. This episode is repeated verbatim in Gloria Fuentes, *La radiodifusión* (Mexico City: Secretaría de Comunicaciones y Transportes, 1987), p. 71, and is also mentioned in Fernando Mejía Barquera, *La industria de la radio y la televisión*, vol. 1 (Mexico City: Fundación Manuel Buendía A.C., 1989), p. 26.

4 *Excélsior*, 18 June 1926, p. 8.

5 "Amundsen y Byrd hacen elogios de *Excélsior*," *Excélsior*, 4 July 1924, p. 1.

6 *Sesión solemne en homenaje al ilustre explorador de los polos Roald Amundsen*, (Mexico City: Sociedad Mexicana de Geografía y Estadística, 1928), p. 135.

GALE FORCES
JACKIE DEE GROM

The McMurdo Dry Valleys of Antarctica are home to one of the most extreme environments in the world—a polar desert blasted by ferocious winds, deprived of all but minimal rain, and beset by a mean annual temperature of negative twenty degrees Celsius. Such conditions are found only here, on a minute portion of the exposed mass of the vast south-ernmost continent, absent of the oppressive ice caps that engulf its remaining expanse.

This harsh setting provides ideal circumstances for the creation of ventifacts, geologic formations shaped by the forces of wind. During the Antarctic summer, from October through February, oceanic winds of ten to fifteen kilometers per hour prevail, but during winter months, gravity-driven winds pour off the high polar plateau, attaining speeds of up to two hundred kilometers per hour. In the grip of these aeolian forces, sand and small pebbles hurl through the air, smashing into volcanic rocks that have fallen from the valley walls, slowly prying individual crystals from their hold, and sculpting natural masterworks over thousands of years. The

multi-directional winds in this eerie and isolated wasteland create ventifacts of an exceptional nature, gouged with pits and decorated with flowing flutes and arching curves.

I came across these ornate vestiges in 2004, as a researcher with the National Science Foundation's Long-Term Ecological Research (LTER) project, led by Peter Doran. My activities in these alien valleys consisted of drilling through three to four meters of ice to retrieve samples from glacial meltwater-fed lakes and maintaining automated weather stations whose data provide a glimpse of the valley's historic and current microclimate. During down times, I'd take a strenuous hike to the terminus of Hughes Glacier, which overlooks the primordial Lake Bonney. There the ventifacts seen heron these pages stood, surveying the land that gave them life. A vast display of volcanic rocks with magmatic intrusions creeping their way up through the skin of our world, it suggested an antiquated planetary vascular system and provided a visual reminder of the extremely violent conditions that created Earth.

Photos Jackie Dee Grom.

the reflected light incorporated them into his dynamic multi-media spectacle. The reviews that followed the New York performance were mixed and inconclusive. Viewers found it difficult to relate the timing and intensity of the colors to the music and one critic dismissed it as "a pretty poppy show."

• • •

The color-music paintings I have made follow Castel (and Kodály) in attempting to make "music for deaf people": abstract works that present a visual installation of silent music. I took Castel's color-keyboard code as the basis for visualizing pitch and devised a second code, which makes visible the tempo of the score. This code takes a crotchet as a certain width, with longer and shorter notes having correspondingly longer or shorter shapes. Each bar is divided horizontally into six lines and there is space for up to three notes in the treble and three notes in the bass clef to be played at any one time.

Each painting starts at the top left of the canvas and works eight bars across, four times, to complete a total of 32 bars. The paintings represent scores from Bach's *Goldberg Variations*. I chose the *Variations* because they were written in the early eighteenth century, and so it is possible that they were played on Castel's ocular harpsichord. Their rich mathematical and harmonic structures would have particularly suited the challenges of such an instrument.

Bach's music can also be linked to the synthesized color sequence in *Close Encounters*. In 1967, the composer and recording artist Wendy Carlos recorded *Switched on Bach* on a Moog synthesizer; the record sleeve shows an actor posing as Bach in eighteenth-century garb and a powdered wig in front of the space-age looking instrument. This famous recording apparently inspired Alan R. Pearlman, who went on to found ARP instruments, one of the seminal synthesizer companies of the 1970s. Pearlman came from a background in classical music and had spent five years working as an engineer designing amplifiers for the Apollo

and Gemini space programs for NASA. It is the ARP 2500 that went on to create synthesizer lore by being used in Spielberg's *Close Encounters*. In the film, the original aspirations of Castel's ocular harpsichord appear to be finally realized. However, when I recently spoke to Philip Dodds, the former ARP engineer who appears in *Close Encounters* as the synthesizer operator, he told me that the synthesizer and light console used in the film were never actually linked.

Inevitably the question remains—are all ocular harpsichords ultimately doomed to failure? Is it possible to create a color-music instrument that will provide a collective sensory experience comparable to what someone with synaesthetic capabilities experiences? Probably not; color-music fascinates because it inhabits the liminal state between two senses, a metaphor for the invisible threads that connect our perception of the world. There is no universal language of color that can be understood on a subliminal level, only a wide range of symbolic associations. Perhaps what the analogy of music and color can allow is a method for translating the subtleties of a musical score and, as Castel originally intended, color-music might be better left as a "thought experiment."

However, there is something attractive about the foolhardy quest for a music of color that appeals to me. These intellectual flights of fantasy teeter like ambitious Towers of Babel in the imagination. Before his death, Scriabin was working towards one such megalomaniacal venture, titled *Mysterium*, which was to be performed in the foothills of the Himalayas. He imagined bells suspended from clouds to summon spectators, sunrises as preludes and sunsets as codas, flames throwing up sheets of fire, and scents choreographed in the air. At the end of the seven-day performance, his antithesis to God's creation, the world was to explode in an apocalyptic flash of mystical bliss.

below: "Musico-Chromo-Logo Schema," the chart of color-sound relationships used for Scriabin's symphony *Prometheus: The Poem of Fire*.

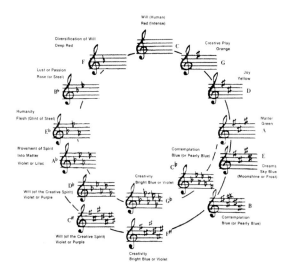

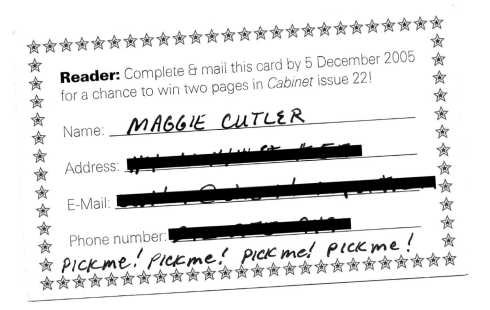

Reader: Complete & mail this card by 5 December 2005 for a chance to win two pages in *Cabinet* issue 22!

Name: *MAGGIE CUTLER*

Address: ▓▓▓▓▓▓▓▓▓▓▓▓▓▓▓

E-Mail: ▓▓▓▓▓▓▓▓▓▓▓▓▓▓▓

Phone number: ▓▓▓▓▓▓▓

pick me! pick me! pick me! pick me!

EDITOR-BY-CHANCE

To be honest, the Grand Lottery Vizier's rather shocking command that our Fall 2005 "Chance" issue include a Crazy Topsy-Turvy Two-Page Reader Giveaway Bonanza-Stravaganza™, was met with some trepidation at the *Cabinet* home office. After all, one of the meager perks allowed those of us who make the magazine is that we generally get to decide what goes into it. Of course, though, when the GLV says jump, one cannot help but ask "how high?" and so we set to the task, establishing the complex administrative regime necessary to govern the enterprise and then waiting, anxiously, for the readers' coupons to roll in. And roll in they did—no fewer than 467 by the given deadline—leaving the Vizier and his minions with the happy, if daunting, task of opening envelopes, deciphering handwriting, pocketing the occasional modest bribe, and then, after fashioning the Choosing Vessel from which the winner would be drawn, placing the entries within said Vessel. Though the tension was thick on the fateful Day of Choosing, all went well and a victor was selected (see <www.cabinetmagazine. org/issues/19/editorbychance.php> for footage of the ceremony).

To the relief of all concerned, that victor turned out to be one Maggie Cutler, a smart and skillful writer from New York City who, after being paid a personal visit by *Cabinet* editors bearing bodega tulips, happily accepted the terms of the endeavor and began her work fully outside our control and sanction. The fascinating results of all this business we are pleased and proud to present, as promised, on the two pages that follow.

CODE ORANGE
MAGGIE CUTLER

The first person to make a mechanical orange was Jean Eugene Robert-Houdin (1805–1871). The illustrious French magician discovered his calling the way I found my way into this issue of *Cabinet*—by chance. As he wrote in his *Confessions*, while still a young clockmaker, he ordered two books on horology from a bookseller who handed him two volumes on magic by mistake. Reading these accidentally acquired manuals, Robert-Houdin foresaw making his mark as a prestidigitator.

Years later, he did. He was the first illusionist to perform on the legitimate stage in evening dress and is often credited with being the first to use modern science in constructing tricks. Robert-Houdin is often called "The Father of Modern Magic," and his stage name, a magical father in its own right, sired Houdini's.

It was in the mid-1800s that Robert-Houdin devised "The Fantastic Orange Tree Trick"—an elaborate piece of stagecraft so well-respected in the trade that as recently as 2002 actor-magician-scholar Ricky Jay re-created it to close his Broadway show, *On the Stem*. The original Fantastic Orange tree apparatus (next page) is in the collection of Christian Fechner, the historian of classical magic. In Fechner's recently published collector's edition of *The Magic of Robert-Houdin, An Artist's Life*, he describes in detail how the trick was performed by one of the illusionist's officially sanctioned successors in the late 1800s. Thanks to Todd Karr of miraclefactory.org who has generously shared his translation of the appropriate passage, here is its gist:

As the magician, you begin by getting a handkerchief from one woman in the audience and a ring from another. Neither are accomplices. You then tie the ring to the handkerchief with a ribbon (to create an ensemble too unique to swap for a look-alike) and you promise to make the handkerchief-ring dematerialize, and then reappear inside an orange. Next, you make an egg vanish into a lemon and that lemon into an orange. But now, you announce, there is no room left in the orange for the handkerchief, so you will have to find some other way to make good on your promise.

Rubbing the egg-lemon-orange in your hands, you reduce it gradually into a powder, which you sprinkle into a liqueur. After your assistant places a potted orange tree on the table beside you, you pour the liqueur into a goblet, light it beneath the orange tree to represent "the heat and light of the sun," and wave your wand, commanding the tree first to flower—which it does—and then to fruit.

"You may think these are mechanical oranges," you say. "Stand corrected, since I will now pick them before your eyes."

After you do, you distribute them to people in the audience to eat.

When only one orange remains, you remind everyone of your promise, saying: "I will take the handkerchief with both my hands and from here I will send it into the orange; I will then tell this orange, 'Open!'"

Fantastically, the orange opens at your command. Two butterflies fly into the air, the original handkerchief and ring between them, whereupon you ask, "Can you see your handkerchief, Madame?" Finally, you return the ring and handkerchief to their respective owners, who confirm your genius by verifying their authenticity.

Robert-Houdin, Fechner explains, originally constructed the final handkerchief-bearing orange in five segments with four hinges, and it "grew" much the same way as the flowers and real oranges did—by being thrust (via cables and levers manipulated by an offstage assistant) from behind various small screens camouflaged with leaves. Still other levers opened the orange and released its mechanical butterflies.

Because the whole mad contraption was the work of a clockmaker and featured an engineered orange, it occurred to me that the penultimate orange on Robert-Houdin's tree may have inspired the person who—back in the days when *queer* meant "odd"—came up with the phrase, "queer as a clockwork orange." It's this bit of folk wit, and not Robert-Houdin's trick, that Anthony Burgess, in various introductions to his dystopian classic, *A Clockwork Orange*, consistently cites as the origin of his novel's title. "Clockwork oranges don't exist," he declares, "except in the speech of old Londoners."

But clockwork oranges *did* exist, and old Londoners were far more likely than Burgess to be aware of them. It's known that the Fantastic Orange Tree Trick was performed and reviewed in late-nineteenth-century London and quite likely later as well. If the origin of "queer as a clockwork orange" coincided with this London engagement, Burgess could have first heard the phrase a mere fifty years later. So it is plausible, however hard to prove, that an ex-clockmaker's fake fruit inspired some Briton's witty metaphor about the incongruity of clocks and oranges—giving Burgess his title. Then again, similarities between the tangible clockwork orange and the verbal one could be a fluke, a chance congruence of ingenious minds. Either way, the trick and the metaphor represent two very different takes on the impact of humans on nature.

There is no record of Robert-Houdin or his audiences perceiving anything "queer" about his mechanical orange. Robert-Houdin most likely featured the orange in his trick because it was naturally segmented and easy to see from the back row. Possibly he knew that some varieties of oranges, unlike most plants, fruit and flower at the same time. The potted orange tree was also in keeping with the high-toned aura of respectability that Robert-Houdin assiduously cultivated. In his delightful book *Oranges* (1966), John McPhee reports that potted orange trees are a relic of the reign of King Charles VIII of France, who, at the end of the fifteenth century, "in an expedition said to mark the dividing point between medieval and modern history," marched off to conquer Italy. Instead, says McPhee, Italian culture conquered Charles and, "when he returned to France, every other man in his retinue was an Italian gardener, an Italian artist or an Italian architect."

Charles's gardeners cultivated Mediterranean oranges at the king's chillier château at Amboise by planting them in pots under mica shelters, and moving them to catch the sun. The *orangerie*, ancestor of the greenhouse, became a staple of royal architecture. Oranges gradually trickled down from the aristocracy to the merchant elite until, in the mid-1800s when Robert-Houdin began performing, they entered middle-class homes. So Robert-Houdin's potted orange tree represented a triumph of horticultural ingenuity and bourgeois cultivation. It was a plant that could quite plausibly cough up a handkerchief and a lady's ring without suffering an identity crisis.

The opposite is true of the English slangster's simile. Whether or not the vivid expression was inspired by a magician's automaton, a metaphorical history of the clockwork orange reveals that somehow the notion of a man-made fruit evolved from a playful nineteenth-century conceit into the epitome of edgy strangeness.

For Burgess in the mid-twentieth century, the idea of authorities reaching into the guts of something natural and manipulating it to suit themselves was the opposite of a parlor trick; it was a kind of ultraviolence. In Malaya, where Burgess had spent time in civil service, he

wrote that the word "orang" meant "human being." To him, the clockwork orange represented "the application of a mechanistic morality to a living organism oozing with juice and sweetness." It was a symbol of Pavlovian humanity, and seemed to him an abominable contradiction in terms.

Today, a "clockwork orange" is no longer a true oxymoron. Genetics and microbiology show us that living things are composed of numerous molecular timers and gizmos that human beings can tweak. Oranges in particular, because they reproduce by apomixis rather than through fertilization, are relatively easy to engineer genetically into little drug and pesticide factories—cornucopias of nourishment and pharmaceuticals for us all—as well as cash cows for the multi-billion-dollar, multinational orange-growing industry. Still, as we know by now, a genetically modified orange is never quite as predictable as clockwork. A part of nature, it is subject to unpredictable environmental interactions, some of which might, by chance, go quite badly. So, when contemplating the future of the orange, Robert-Houdin's evocation of wonder and Burgess's dread both seem fully apt, leaving most of us with that stroboscopic ambivalence best described in the phrase of the anonymous poet, as "queer as a clockwork orange."

This issue marks the first in a series of ongoing collabora-
tions between *Cabinet* and *Implicasphere*, an occasional
periodical created by the London-based editorial collaborative of Cathy Haynes and Sally O'Reilly. Although their
formats may be different, *Cabinet* and *Implicasphere* are
kindred spirits—both freely mixing textual and image-based
material around a chosen theme, both drawing on a range
of disciplines and scholarship, both surveying the margins
of history and culture for signs of pattern and affinity. Past
issues of *Implicasphere* have examined topics such as Mice,
Folly, and String—for their initial volume in our pages, they
tackle the Nose.

For information and to purchase back issues of *Implicasphere*, email
<info@implicasphere.org.uk> or visit <www.implicasphere.org.uk>.

remove gently

TO BE OR A KNOT TO BE

CHRISTINE WERTHEIM

"To be, or not to be." The most famous words in the English canon. But *what*, exactly, is the question? For Hamlet it appeared as a matter of life or death, but in modernists such as Samuel Beckett, Thomas Bernhard, and Elfriede Jelinek, we encounter situations in which, though the "I" of the text is clearly alive, it finds itself, in some way, radically negated. In such states, it is not clear that there is any substantial difference between being and not being. Faced with this thoroughly modern dilemma, how might we proceed?

As this is a problem of both being *and* language, perhaps we should begin with the words. "To be, or not to be: that is the question." We have already seen that in existential soul-searching, the shift to modernity requires, in the second half of the proposed dilemma, the substitution of a *w* for the *t*. This shift produces the new formulation, "To be, or not to be: *what* is the question?", the problem no longer being whether to simply be here or not, but whether we can still say that there is any real difference between these apparent choices. If the second half of the assertion has undergone a semantic shift, might not the first part also require modification if it is to adequately register the most recent findings in how we define subjectivity? In line with this hypothesis, might we not propose that the thoroughly twenty-first century version of Hamlet's dilemma is: "To be or a kNot to be: what is the question?" And the question is: What *is* the question here?

Clearly, our updated formulation of the existential dilemma is rather complex, not to say, positively paradoxical. We should not then be surprised that there is no general consensus on what is at stake in this question, let alone anything like an agreement on an appropriate method for addressing it. However, many notable writers, poets, philosophers, and social theorists have put their critical capacities to work on the problem. Of this plethora, one of the more intriguing is that proposed by the French psychoanalyst Jacques Lacan.

THE LACANIAN SUBJECT: REAL, SYMBOLIC, AND IMAGINARY

> In the beginning was what's kNot.
> Then God said, "Let the kNot be."
> And It was.
> And It was a Borromean Knot.

Though Lacan's approach to the analysis of the psyche was originally inspired by the anthropologist Claude Lévi-Strauss, who had successfully applied group theory to the analysis of kinship systems, and more contentiously to myths, Lacan was no ordinary structuralist, and could not stop at mere group theory. Appropriating geometry, topology, and eventually knot theory for his notion of the psyche, in the early 1970s Lacan settled on a model in which psychic reality is (re)presented as a complex of three separate, but interrelated spheres: the Real, the Symbolic, and the Imaginary.

In this model, the three rings do not represent boundaries of areas on the plane; the figure is not a set diagram. Rather, the rings represent *rims*, or holes in a "body," around which desire flows. Lacan's idea here is that the psyche is itself a "body" or space whose boundaries are defined by its rims, just as we can say that, from a topological perspective, the space of the physical body is defined by the rims of its orifices—the mouth, nostrils, eye-sockets, ear-holes, anus, and vagina. The difference with psychic-body space is that its rims are not dispersed across a surface, but are twined into a "knot," which lies at the center of the being. The figure that these rims form, the navel of Lacan's psyche, is known technically as a Borromean knot.

THE BORROMEAN

The Borromean knot is composed of three rings linked in such a way that no two alone are connected. Only when all three come together does the linkage occur. In this case, to undo one is to undo them all.[1] This three-in-one feature of the Borromean perhaps explains its pervasive use in the religious systems of many otherwise vastly different cultures.

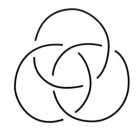

As Colin C. Adams states in the *Knot Book*, his enormously accessible and erudite introduction to knots, in contemporary mathematical parlance, knots are objects composed of a single "closed curve in space that does not intersect itself anywhere."[2] Objects like the Borromean, which are composed of *more than one* interlinked element, are thus not technically knots but rather "links." However, the longevity of the Borromean figure's designation as a knot means that it is interchangeably known as the Borromean knot, the Borromean link, and even the Borromean rings. The shape of the rings does not effect the configuration. They can be round or square, made of DNA chains, laurel branches, or lines in hyperspace. What matters is simply that "to undo one is to undo them all." We may also add a *fourth* ring to the configuration, to derive a figure known as the Borromean lock, a figure to which we will return later. Interestingly, though Borromeans *seem* to occur in both two and three dimensions, in reality, they are all three-dimensional. The two-dimensional version is just an image, a *projection* or shadow, of the three-dimensional form.

Whatever its technical designation, the adjective "Borromean" derives from the object's association with the family of Borromeo who added the three-ringed link to their crest in the fourteenth century. In the early-fifteenth century, when Francesco Sforza, who had inherited the family's estates, was made Duke of Milan, he gave permission to other noble families to use it on their crests, as a sign of his expanding domain, though technically it designates only the region around Cremona. Consequently, the rings can be found on many monuments in and around Milan: inside and outside, on floors and ceilings, in the shapes of the windows, and engraved on architraves. Sforza Castle, Francesco's elaborately fortified manse, is covered in them, though photography is not allowed on the premises.

But long before this aristocratic family co-opted the form, its image had appeared in many cultures around the globe and across the ages, in particular in connection with religious beliefs and practices. "A form of the Borromean link was used by the Norse people of Scandinavia. The symbol known as 'Odin's triangle' or the 'Walknot' (meaning 'knot of the slain') has two variants. One is a set of Borromean triangles; the other is a unicursal curve that forms a trefoil knot. ... [It] is associated with the Norse god Odin. Scenes on picture stones show fallen warriors traveling to the next world by boat or on horseback where they will join others in Odin's palace, Valhalla—the castle of the slain. Hovering in space above the dead, the Borromean/Walknot signifies the passage to this 'other' place."[3]

For many centuries now, the Borromean rings have also been used to depict the mystery of the Christian Trinity. "The earliest source for this that we are aware of was a thirteenth-century manuscript in the Municipal Library at Chartres. It contained four diagrams. ... In the centre, inside all the circles, is the word 'unitas'; the three syllables of 'tri-ni-tas' are distributed in the outer sectors."[4] Borromeans have also been found in non-western cultures such as that of the Shinto religion in Japan, whose mythology divides the world into three realms: heaven (the land of gods), earth (the land of man), and the underworld (land of the dead). Their interconnectedness is represented by the three interlinked circles, which can be found all over ancient Shinto shrines such as O-Miwa Jinja. Lately, Borromean-like figures have also been found in natural phenomena, e.g., the molecular structure of certain chemical substances. But though the figure, and many other different kinds of knots and links, have appeared in a wide variety of cultures and conditions, it was not until the late-nineteenth century that mathematicians began to study them seriously.[5] Now more than a century old, knot theory is one of the most dynamic areas of modern mathematics. The study of knots has led to important applications in the synthesis of new molecules and in DNA research, and is now widely used in statistical mechanics and quantum field theory. It can also help us further our understanding of the psychic cosmos.

PSYCHOANALYSIS AND THE DENOUEMENT

One of the most fascinating facts about knots is that, if cut, they can be tied together to produce other knots.[6] This process is rather like doing arithmetic. Such processes can also be performed with links. However, sometimes the operation causes an element to become unlinked, that is, to fall out. From the 1970s on, Lacan conceived of analytic practice as quite literally a topological operation in which the knot of the analysand's psyche is tied to the knot of the analyst, in order that something troubling to the analysand can drop out. In order to understand how this might work, we must first consider how the analytic "symptom" is positioned within the psyche as a whole.

We have already seen how in Lacan's original knotty model, the psyche is (re)presented as a space bounded by the three interlocked rings of the Real, Symbolic, and Imaginary. However, in 1975, after his long encounter with the writings of James Joyce, Lacan felt compelled to add a fourth ring to the configuration, turning it from a link into a lock. Called the *sinthome* (one of Lacan's many plays on words), this fourth element—the symptom—is what keeps a psyche locked up. From this perspective, the aim of Lacanian analysis is to unlock the link by breaking the *sinthome*'s hold—that is, to untie the fourth ring and let the psyche be, as simply as it can, a three-ring knot. "To be knotted otherwise, this is what is essential to the Oedipus Complex and it is precisely [this on which] analysis operates."[7]

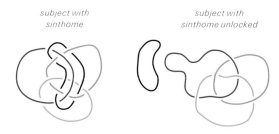

subject with
sinthome

subject with
sinthome unlocked

Analysis then, as a practice, rather than a theory, is for Lacan simply the operation of this unlocking—the separation of the *sinthome* from the body of the psychic link. The analytic situation may thus be represented by a diagram in which two Borromean knots—a lock and a link—are conjoined.

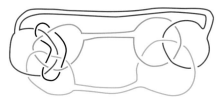

the analytic situation

The knot, on the right, represents the analyst who, having herself already shed her *sinthome*, has only three rings in play. The other, on the left, is the analysand, whose *sinthome* is still locked into the subject. In an article entitled "The Topological Dénouement of the Cure," the analyst/mathematician Robert Groome states that this configuration can be topologically transformed—morphed without cutting—into two Borromean links, with the fourth ring of the analysand's *sinthome* dropping out in the process.[8]

In other words, according to Groome, the analytic cure is a *topological operation* in which two knots join so that one can become unlocked. As Groome nicely phrases it, this unlocking process of separation is not a negative experience, but a "positive moment of *dé-nouement.*" However, this denouement does not render the analysand tangle-free, insofar as what is left is still a knot, or at least a link. Furthermore, the ring of the *sinthome* does not disappear; it simply detaches itself from the other psychic rims. In this way, we may say that the analytic operation does not free one *from* entanglements; rather, it frees one *into* a new kind of knot, one that is structured as a link, not a lock. But if the psyche as a whole is composed of a space plus its boundaries, and if these boundaries can be reconfigured by topological operations, does this mean that the boundaries and the space they define represent two different psychic phenomena? And how does this relate to the tripartite division between Real, Symbolic, and Imaginary?

From the perspective of mathematical theory, knots—which for the purposes of this argument will be taken to include links and locks—are not essentially conceived as holes in space. Rather a knot is a logically autonomous entity that can be studied quite independently of any space in which it may be embedded. However, *knots may also be used to construct different spaces*. When we do this, the knot is not considered as a hole cut in the space, but rather, as alluded to above, is seen as the *boundary by which the space is defined*. A space defined by a knot, including links and locks, is known technically as a knot-complement. A knot complement is what's left when a knot is either entirely removed from a space, or pushed away to infinity. The latter case does not lead to a situation in which, if we just kept going, somewhere out there, we'd finally run into a giant knot. The space is called a knot-complement because the knot has *effectively* been removed from it (the result of shoving it off to infinity). No matter how long you traveled, or how fast, you would never reach the rings of the knot itself. As you headed for where these would be, distances that look small to an external observer would actually become extremely large and you would never reach the edge.[9] There is now intense mathematical interest in knot-complements, because they have amazing properties. Borromean knots also have complements, but before investigating the specific qualities of such a space, we should first make a more clear distinction between the knot and its complement in Lacan's topological model of the psyche. In other words, we must now make a clear distinction between the psyche in general, and that specific psychic phenomenon that Lacan called the "Subject."

In much of his writing, Lacan refers to the Subject as a rim, or edge-condition, around which desire flows. If we combine this notion with the hypothesis of his topological model of analysis, we see that, for Lacan, the Subject is the "rim" or "edge" of the psychic-body space. The "Subject" is the limit-condition where the body of psychic space encounters its own discrete boundaries. In other words, the "Subject" is nothing but the "event" of the psyche becoming aware of its own limits, this event taking place around a rim knotted into the form of a Borromean. If the Subject is thus the knot itself, the knot-complement is an analyzed psyche *minus* the Subject, that is to say, a psyche that has both shed its *sinthome* and withdrawn from its fixation on its self. What would be the experience of subsisting in such a space?

NOT KNOT: THE FILM

In their bamboozling and thoroughly enlightening film, *Not Knot*, the mathematicians David Epstein and Charlie Gunn of the Geometry Center at the University of Minnesota use computer graphics to take us on a guided tour of a Borromean knot-complement. But, as they explain, in order to truly appreciate its wonders, we must first get some idea of how such a space may actually be constructed; that is to say, we need a more thorough understanding than merely the knowledge that it can be described as a space with a knot taken out.

The following sequence describes the steps used in the film to arrive at this knowledge.[10]

1. Imagine the Euclidean space we have all been taught to regard as the model of our physical universe—homogeneous, three-dimensional, stretching infinitely in all directions.

2. Mold this space into a ball. It's still infinitely wide in every direction; it just has a spherical shape. (Technically, to actually do this, we would first have to add a point. As this is just a teensy-weensy dimensionless point, we'll just consider it done and carry on.)

3. Deform the ball to make a cube.

4. Draw a line, or axis, down the middle of each side of the cube:

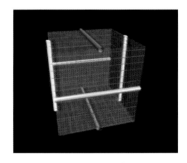

5. Bend each pair of sides so that their two axes join into a loop. The result is a space bounded by three rings linked into a Borromean knot. Note that this knot lies not on the inside of the space but at its outermost edges:

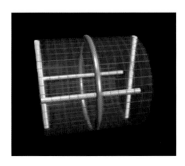

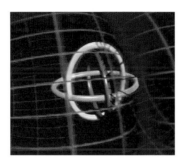

Now comes the tricky part!

6. Imagine that each of these three boundary lines functions as what mathematicians call an "axis of symmetry." In other words, as well as having the shape of a ring, each axis now acts like a mirror, bouncing back light rays that hit it. Note that these "mirrors" do not lie within the space; they are located as its boundaries. Thus, a light-ray reaching the ends of this space bounces back, giving the illusion that space has been doubled. Remember, too, that we have three of these mirror boundaries and that each has the shape of a self-enclosed ring.

7. Turning on one symmetry axis of our deformed cube produces the appearance of an infinite row of boxes.

8. Turning on two axes of symmetry produces an infinite plane of cubes:

9. Switching on all three axes gives the illusion of an infinite volume tiled by cubes, very much like sitting in a Yayoi Kusama Infinity Box:

10. Now repeat steps 3–9, only begin by molding the sphere into a dodecahedron...

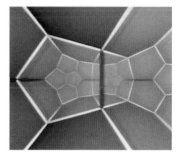

11. ...while also giving each axis the power of four-fold symmetry, rather than the simple doubling capacity of normal mirrors. Note that mathematical "mirrors" are not limited to one reproduction of space (as in our material world), but may reflect many times, depending on the "symmetry" properties of the mirror. A picture of the resultant space would have a pseudo-crystalline structure in which each cell is a duplicate of the original dodecahedral form:

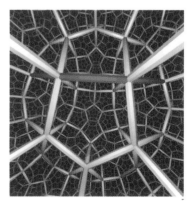

Such a space would be of finite volume and possibly quite small in relation to the spatial scales commonly associated with cosmological models, and it would contain a limited number of galaxies. But the multi-connected nature of this space would present a virtually unlimited number of images of these galaxies, often referred to as "ghosts." To an even greater extent than gravitational mirages, these topological

mirages would create a vast optical illusion, making space appear much bigger than it really is. [11]

This is what happens when we have four-fold symmetry. Is it possible that our axes can be given even more reflecting power? Say 10, 11, 20, 1000-fold symmetry? What about infinite reflectivity? As it happens, the answer to this question is yes, if we allow that the space occupied by our dodecahedron can be *hyperbolic*, rather than Euclidean. [12] In this case, if we keep decreasing the angles at its vertices indefinitely, the axes of reflection are pushed further and further away, causing the symmetry to increase.

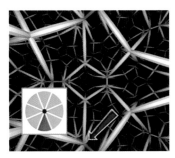

When the axes are pushed to infinity, the symmetries also become infinite. The final sequences of *Not Knot* give us a virtual tour through just such a universe. As we revolve through the space, the points at infinity seem to come closer and closer. Then, just as we expect them to hit us in the eye, they suddenly swerve round the back of our head, and a new vista, with vast bundles of rays receding into the infinite, opens again before us. *This* is what it's like to be inside the complement of a Borromean knot.

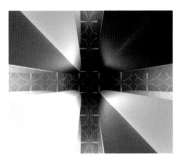

Although, at the small local level, lived experience offers little support for the idea that the real world conforms to this strange geometry, some scientists have dreamed that at the overall macro level, it might. Sadly, a probe now sending information back from the outer reaches of the cosmos suggests that this is probably not the case. But, if the psyche, *sans* Subject, i.e., minus an awareness of its own limits, is the complement of the Borromean knot, then psychic space is precisely that described in *Not Knot*. Thus, if we wish to take a hyperbolic trip, all we have to do, apart from slipping out of our *sinthomes*, is to withdraw from our fixation on our selves, and relax into the sublime fantasy of a limitless void. Maybe the mystics got it right after all.

1 Other versions of the three-ring pattern exist, but these are not "true" or *mathematical* Borromeans. See the Borromean Rings Homepage <www.liv.ac.uk/~spmr02/rings/>.

2 Colin C. Adams, *The Knot Book: An Elementary Introduction to the Theory of Knots* (New York: W. H. Freeman and Company, 1994), p. 2.

3 Ibid.

4 Ibid.

5 For an introduction to the mathematical study of knots, links, locks, and braids, see Margaret Wertheim, "Where the Wild Things Are: An Interview with Ken Millett," in *Cabinet* no. 20.

6 Ibid.

7 Lacan, "R.S.I.," 14 January 1975, quoted from the website of P.L.A.C.E. <www.topoi. net/place6/logic.LonFigure.html>. I am indebted for this insight to the seminars given by P.L.A.C.E. (Psychoanalysis Los Angeles California Extension), a non-profit association that provides a framework permitting a de-medicalization and de-therapeutization of the analytic process. For more information, visit <www.topoi.net>.

8 Robert Groome, "The Topological Dénouement of the Cure," <www.topoi.net/place6/logic.LonFigure.html>.

9 Colin C. Adams, *The Knot Book: An Elementary Introduction to the Theory of Knots*, op. cit., pp. 245–246.

10 The instructions here are my abbreviated interpretation of the second half of the film *Not Knot*, made by The Geometry Center, University of Minnesota, in 1990 and published by A. K. Peters, Ltd.

11 Marc Lachieze-Rey and Jean-Pierre Luminet, *Celestial Treasury*, trans. Joe Laredo (Cambridge: Cambridge University Press, 2001), p. 45.

12 See Margaret Wertheim, "Crocheting the Hyperbolic Plane," in *Cabinet* no. 16.

opposite: a cross-cultural selection of Borromean knots. From top:

1. Japanese family crest.

2. Japanese family crest featuring the comma-shaped *tomoe*, a common design element in Japanese family emblems.

3. Detail sketch of the third panel of the Larbro picture stone (ca. ninth century) showing a Viking *Valknut* (Walknot) or "knot of the slain." The six-panel stone, which seems to depict an offering to Odin, is located on Gotland, an island in the Baltic sea off the southeast coast of Sweden.

4. The door of the Church of San Sigismondo in Cremona, where Bianca Maria Visconti and Francesco Sforza were married in 1441. Sforza's family emblems, including the Borromean rings, are carved on the door. Photo Peter Cromwell.

5. Motif on courtyard wall of the Palazzo Borromeo in Milan. Photo Peter Cromwell.

A BRIEF HISTORY OF THE FUTURE
ALAN BERGER & DORION SAGAN

Failure is more beautiful than success.
　　—John Fante

1. Ruination has its metaphysical and cosmological, as well as its personal and physical, aspects.

2. Metaphysically, ruination is in stark contrast, almost a mocking antithesis, to the timeless realm accessible by mathematical imagination, Platonic speculation, and mystic reports. The fact that a distant supernova has ceased to exist by the time the light from its explosion reaches our eyes alerts us that we may ourselves be misperceived as present whereas in reality we are only the physical afterimage of a previous phenomenon. Projecting forward in time, the immediate present becomes, as Nabokov pointed out, a future memory, such that our present life, with its blue jeans and magazines, its global economy and media, becomes, from the vantage point of the future, a quaint throwback to a serene yesteryear, a 3-D daguerreotype. (Nabokov adds that such a prolepsis, turning ordinary things into invaluable, active antiques, living cultural fossils, enhances the aesthetics of daily life.) In quantum mechanics, physicist John Wheeler suggests that it is the presence in the future of far more numerous observers that co-creates the present reality in which we find ourselves. If time is, as Wheeler's colleague Einstein put it in a letter to the family of a dead friend, a "persistent illusion," then the very category of ruination is suspect, because everything already is. The Hindu solution, too anthropomorphic to be fully scientific, is that the Godhead, bored with eternity, creates the illusion (*maya*) of passing time, of separation into discrete individuals, mortals, to keep himself occupied. The whole must be split in space, rifted in time, in order to perceive itself at all. But then why *this* particular configuration, this set-up? Something doesn't add up, unless, as co-author Nabokov hinted, the first author had a particular whimsical and not uncruel sense of humor.

3. But perhaps this world is best described neither by science nor religion, neither by cosmology, which posits billions of years of becoming (and thus inevitable ruin as the new replaces the old) from the big bang through microbial and human evolution, nor by the antiseptic eternities of the Platonic imagination, be they mathematical or Christian. Perhaps this world is neither natural nor supernatural

Figure 1: A landfill in Buford, Georgia.

Figure 2: Plane disaster scene set, *War of the Worlds*, Universal Studios, Hollywood, California.

Figure 3: Rail hub. Norfolk Southern's Inman Yard and CSX's Tilford Yard, Atlanta, Georgia.

1.

4.

5.

6.

but rather both, which is to say Todorovian after Tzvetan Todorov's literary category of the *fantastique*, which simultaneously admitted of natural and supernatural explanations. The helpful mystic Ouspensky says in his 1911 *Tertium Organum, Or The Third Canon Of Thought And A Key To The Enigmas Of The World* that the difference between a building and an idea is that (we paraphrase) buildings can be bombed while attempts to take down, to destroy, an idea only underline its importance, making it stronger. Witness Christianity, let alone the twin towers crucified and yet simultaneously raised up, lifted, and preserved at a higher level by the real-world equivalent of the Hegelian *Aufhebung*.

4. We ourselves are partly ruined and ruinous beings, feeding on energy and fomenting destruction, leaving in our wake complexity free of a sense of divine design. In this, we resemble other natural complex systems—organized by energy flow and described in thermodynamics as helping to disperse energy, break down a gradient, or produce entropy. From its possible beginnings in ocean floor vents captured so well in James Cameron's 3-D film, *Aliens of the Deep*—the *mise-en-scène* evokes a mutant recrudescence of Bosch's creatures lost at sea—life has been destroying one thing to create another, chewing up light to spit out microgreenery, availing itself of chemistry to internally quiver and grow, tapping into energy to imagine the blueprint, secrete the solid waste, or power the crane.

5. In time, at least, there is no site in end. These wrecking balls and chimneys keep stomping and coughing, burying most of the present at its birth, but leaving a venous veil visible to the watchful artistic eye, so that it might contemplate in vision the eloquent words of the Italian philosopher Maurizio Ferraris: "In what sense 'is there' a star that exploded a thousand years ago, and that we see now? … It is to be noted that, according to the distinction between phenomenon and noumenon, everything visible—ourselves included—could be nothing but memory and phenomenalization, no less than stars that have exploded, and appeared precisely when they have ceased to be noumena."

6. And it is true that we do not know that this work, so real and full of designs, though not those of a straight-thinking creator or narrator, is not already destroyed, and that these our lives, amid the ruins of the present, are not part of a more rapturous edifice accruing to that vision which contains all things in a necessarily more bland eternity.

Text by Dorion Sagan. Photographs by Alan Berger.

Figure 4: Plastid-implanted hillocks adjacent to housing in Irvine, California.
Figure 5: Car salvage and junkyard near Ayer, Massachusetts. In 2003, over twelve million automobiles were scrapped or junked in the US.
Figure 6: Interchange at Interstate Highway 210 and Interstate Highway 15, San Bernadino, California.

RE-USE VALUE
JENNY TOBIAS

Consider this image. It's clearly a turn-of-the-century studio portrait, but what else is it? To a stock photography agency, it could be an umbrella ad, a calendar illustration, or a costume designer's reference. To one agency, it's identified as:

☐ 1	☐ Europeans	☐ Jewish	☐ Prominent persons
☐ Americans	☐ Full-length portraits	☐ Males	☐ Studio portraits
☐ Archivist	☐ Full-length studio portraits	☐ Otto L. Bettmann	☐ Toddler
☐ Baby	☐ Germans	☐ People	☐ Umbrella
☐ Boys	☐ Holding	☐ Portraits	☐ Whites
☐ Children			

According to the original caption, it is also a *Portrait of Otto Bettmann—About 2 Years of Age, With an Umbrella*.

Little Otto in his skirts could not have known that he would start collecting images as a teenager, earn a Ph.D. at twenty-five, begin compiling a picture history of civilization while curator of rare books in the Prussian State Art Library in Berlin, flee Nazism to the United States in 1935, and shortly thereafter found the Bettmann Archive, a major purveyor of stock photography. Nor did he know that sixty years after its founding, the Archive would be acquired by Microsoft's Bill Gates for his Corbis image archive, shipped from lower Manhattan to a climate-controlled Pennsylvania mountain for preservation and digitization, and then redistributed over the Internet, where little Otto can be found today, exactly a century after the photographer snapped the shutter.

Stock photography plays a role in all contemporary media, from print to cinema to television, from the analogue to the digital (including computer games). It appears in news and entertainment media, and in commercial, literary, and scholarly publishing. It's also intertwined with art photography, because artists both produce and use stock imagery. In the categorizing spirit of the industry, let's define stock as the commercially motivated creation, collection, organization, and/or dissemination of professional but anonymous or corporatized images. Stock increasingly includes photojournalistic, moving-image, art historical, and fully computer-generated work—and even audio clips. One need only start reading photo credits to discover stock's pervasiveness. No credit? That's often stock too, at several removes from its origin. Like émigré Otto.

Pervasive but uncredited—this is also the place of stock in the history of photography. Yet, through its visual power and ubiquity, stock photography has played an important, if unwitting, role in promulgating new assumptions (or anxieties) about media in general and photography in particular. Over the past hundred years, stock's consumers—we, the media-literate public—have come to terms with concepts that are as fundamental to the stock industry as to theories of the postmodern image. Specifically: photographs have no "essential" meaning or inherent truth; commerce, journalism, and art are deeply interrelated; authorship is fluid; and imagery of the past is integral to image-making in the present and future. Bettmann's baby picture is a good example. The multiple categories defining his portrait demonstrate stock agencies' understanding that images carry meaning far beyond the photographer's intention and any inherent photographic truth. For example, nothing in this image itself denotes *Jewish*, which, like *Whites*, functions in the typological list more as a fraught social designation than as a visual cue. To contemporary eyes, moreover, the image could as easily be filed under *Girls* as *Boys*, while only in retrospect do the terms *Prominent Persons* and *Archivist* apply. *German* and *American*, similarly, may account for Bettmann's émigré experience, but are hardly legible in the image. Yet, oddly, in listing all this detail, no descriptor fixes the picture in its era. To the stock industry, images are timeless because they are mutable.

As Bettmann recounts in his lively memoir *Bettmann: The Picture Man*, his pictorial history of civilization—which evolved into the Archive—entailed, among other methods of image-capture, the photographic cropping of famous artworks into decontextualized, freely circulating signs. A 1932 catalogue card, for example, shows a detail of *Saint Lucas*

Writing Material	C. 4/17　　Leica
	Nr.　　Format
	Rogier van der **Weyden** (1400-1464) Saint Lucas drawing Madonna.　Detail. Munich.　Gallery
Subjects: Drawing hands artist silverpoint pergament	aufgenommen: 14. 7. 1932 Bemerkungen: Ref.: Max J. Friedlander Geschichte der altniederld. Malerei. 1923 ff
Bildarchiv Dr. Otto Bettmann, Berlin	

Drawing Madonna (ca. 1450) by Rogier van der Weyden. Under the general heading *Writing Material*, various subjects are parsed and cross-referenced: *Drawing*, *Hands*, *Artist*, *Silverpoint*, and *Pergament* (parchment). Such content-driven categorization would become key to the Archive's commercial future, as a writer for the magazine *P.M.* foresaw just months after Bettmann arrived in the US:

> *This collection has not been made as an art collection. Subject matter is the foremost consideration ... [He] makes it possible to press the painters of old ... into service as illustrators.*

In this way, the early business habits of stock agencies anticipated the postmodern understanding that images constitute "floating signs" in which meaning can be determined only in context.

As a product for sale, stock's context is consumer desire, and the index of this interest is the agency classification system. How do people search for images—that is, how do they locate in the plethora of available goods the particular picture-commodity they wish to buy? A 2001 micro-study in *Creative Review*, a publication serving the advertising and graphic design industry, reflects the often clumsy process of matching a general idea to a particular representation. In the informal, month-long survey of stock agencies, top search categories included *Baby*, *Business*, *Computer/s*, *Family*, *Flower/s*, *Internet*, *Water*, *Woman/en*, and the more specialized science-photo category *Human Body*. (Oddly, *Man* was a top search at only one agency, less popular than *Money* or *Dog*.) The survey suggests that the search process tends to begin with simple nouns like these, and end with subtle abstractions. For example, Getty customers who searched on their own most often queried *People*, *Business*, or *Computer*, while the most frequent searches mediated by a stock-agency rep were *Escapism*, *Absence*, *Cut Out*, *Nobody*, *Strategy*, *Afterlife*, *Role Reversal*, and *Communication Problems*. Because of this unstable relationship between ideas and images, categorizing is the focus of much research and development in the world of stock, and "keyword" is now a verb. Keywording writes the new master narrative.

Master narratives of photography's history, however, are only now recognizing stock photography. Long marginalized along with that of most commercial photography, the history of stock photography is as fragmented as its images. Still, historians who have tackled the subject seem to agree on four elements central to stock's development: the professionalization of photography, advertising, and modeling—especially modeling by women—in the late nineteenth century; the popularity of photographic entertainments like the stereoscope; the rise of the picture press in the early twentieth century; and the sheer magnitude of stock itself—the quantities of photographs available for use and reuse.

In the twentieth century, stock emerged as a discrete commercial practice. Of agencies that have been studied, sales records from the H. Armstrong Roberts agency date to 1913, and it published a catalogue in 1920 that is believed to be the first of its kind. The Black Box studio in New York and Photographic Advertising Limited in London were selling stock by the early 1930s, and the Bettmann Archive was founded in late 1935, less than a year before the debut of *Life* magazine. By mid-century, stock agencies were integral to journalism and advertising. Culver Pictures, prominent through the 1950s, was born of just such a confluence: working at a Philadelphia newspaper in the 1920s, D. Jay Culver repurposed unused publicity photographs, reselling them as photo essays to New York magazines. As television and other non-print media became prominent, successful stock agencies reinvented themselves to suit. Beginning in the late 1980s, intense consolidation resulted in mega-

opposite: "Portrait of Otto Bettmann—About 2 Years of Age, With an Umbrella." Available through Corbis for a fee.

above: Bettmann Archive catalogue card, 1932.

agencies, notably Getty Images, which now commands 70 million visual assets, having acquired major stock archives and similar repositories of audio, film, art, sports, news, and celebrity photography. Its holdings include Time-Life images as well as the major collection of British photojournalism, the Hulton Archive. Whatever the medium, the first century of stock is the history of speculative interrelationships between journalism, art, and commerce, in which a source can be a client, a client can be a source, and sources might be once or twice removed from their original context.

Thus, by the 1980s, Barbara Kruger, Richard Prince, and other media-conscious artists of the "Pictures Generation" had almost a century of journalistic and commercial photography to mine for their investigations of the generic image. Their works questioned notions of originality, as well as the gender and ethnic stereotypes perpetuated by stock photography. And of course, advertising itself soon re-incorporated the postmodern lessons of media appropriation and recontextualization. Addressing the interconnectedness of art and commerce, in the early 1990s artist and designer Tibor Kalman edited *Colors*, an advertisement in the form of a magazine published by the Benetton clothing company. *Colors* made extensive use of stock, with particular emphasis on recontextualization. Kalman claimed to use photography to show that "you have to learn (and then teach others) to mistrust everything. ... To be responsible, those of us who work in the media have to tell people not to believe in us."

Arguably, a proportion of media consumers today have learned this lesson precisely because of these powerful deployments of stock photography, resulting in a kind of media-savvy available even to primary school children: a knowing attitude towards the fluidity of fact and fiction, news and entertainment, art and commerce. Of course, such cynicism does not readily translate into immunity from advertising's influence. *Colors* stimulated an unusual amount of public debate about photojournalistic manipulation and sensationalism, much of it focused on explicitly altered images (such as Queen Elizabeth Photoshopped with Asian features). Ironically, debate about *Colors* became a media event in itself, much of it sensationalist: Kalman achieved his goal. For while photojournalism still carries the baggage of objectivity, stock is manipulative by definition. For example, in stock's copyright-casual early days, rights were often sold to a corporate body, abandoned, ignored, or lost through successive appropriations. Images would also often be further decontextualized through re-captioning, cropping, "ghosting" and "silhouetting," in which the central image is isolated from its background.

Sometimes, though, the author refuses to give up the ghosting. Consider Barbara Kruger's 1990 silkscreen *Untitled (It's a Small World But Not If You Have to Clean It)*. Anyone acquainted with the artist's work would assume that the photograph is an anonymous image drawn from an advertisement, picture library, or stock agency. Anyone, that is, except for Magnum photographer Thomas Höpker and his subject, Charlotte Dabney, who sued Kruger for appropriating *Charlotte, As Seen By Thomas*

(ca. 1959), charging copyright infringement, "unfair competition," and violation of Dabney's civil right to privacy by making her "a public spectacle."

For Dabney and Höpker, *Charlotte, As Seen by Thomas* remained the inalienable work of one photographer and one subject. But *Charlotte* was seen in a slightly different way by the editors of the German photography magazine *Foto Prisma*, which published it in 1960, and in another by Kruger, who thirty years later appropriated the shot from an unknown source and cropped it into politically charged art. It was then seen by museums as a promotional tool: for Kruger's traveling retrospective in 1999–2000, the work was manufactured into everything from refrigerator magnets to a five-story billboard. In the end, the suit was thrown out on a significant technicality: copyright law changed—and changed back—at key moments, placing *Charlotte* in the US public domain between 1988 and 1994.

In this context, authorship is ultimately a function of international copyright law, and authorship plays a much greater role in the stock industry today, in the era of Disney-driven copyright extension. Because rights management can inhibit use (ask any scholar or publisher), the stock industry has responded with lucrative "rights-free" collections. These themed image collections (often pre-silhouetted) are sold once for unlimited use by the buyer.

Yet an equally strong industry trend concerns new claims to authorship and identity, with recognizably "name brand" sources like Tony Stone Images (now owned by Getty) in demand as an alternative to truly generic, anonymous-looking stock. Max Zerrahn's *A woman holding a magnifying glass to her eye* (undated) from the stock agency fStop/Veer embraces the snapshot aesthetic, grunge fashion, and quasi-portraiture. Not only is the photographer named; we learn that "Max plays guitar in the Indiepop band Solarscape."

Works like this not only re-appropriate for the commercial market the aesthetics of Nan Goldin and Cindy Sherman, but commodify the "lifestyle" and politics of their images as well. On the other hand, the work represents a new legitimacy for unapologetically "commercial art." One might even call it Realist Capitalism: the frank embrace of photography's role in a larger socio-economic system.

The art-stock model also operates in reverse: stock-photo morgues are being reanimated by the marketing of selected images as art. Such newly reclaimed images include nostalgic sports photojournalism and pictures by renowned Works Progress Administration photographers. *The New York Times*, for example, proudly advertises that "our historic photographs, with traditional frames, grace the walls of hotels, hospitals, government agencies, law firms, galleries, financial institutions and celebrities' homes." Of course, this art-commerce interconnection may be newly lucrative, but it is not entirely new: legendary art/commercial photographer and curator Edward Steichen had wallpaper for his home made from a musical motif supplied by Bettmann. Even Bettmann's baby picture has come full circle: in the Corbis era, the one transaction on record for this image is for "personal use," which to a company rep means "to hang on the wall in your house or something." Thus a personal portrait was put into commercial service, then eventually became domestic art.

The stock industry thrives on this art-commerce-journalism mix. Heightened contemporary awareness of this interrelationship has, arguably, fostered new interest in works evoking what we like to think of as the pre-critical period, a time of more innocent image consumption. This can be seen in the current popularity of "naive" commercial photography, which takes on a new light in comparison to the critical meta-photography of the Pictures Generation. For example, *Portrait of a Man Holding Up Magnifying Glass* (undated) is distributed by Retrofile.com, an agency focused precisely on this "retro" market niche. Similar interest now embraces other types of stock media, such as "library music" and "clip art." In the stock industry, a commonplace is the "twenty-year" rule, the age at which culture attains camp status and therefore becomes re-marketable. As Bettmann himself said, "I hate nostalgia but I've made a hell of a living from it."

And what of the future of this past? When Corbis purchased the Bettmann Archive in 1995, sixty years after its founding and three years before Bettmann's death, it heralded the incorporation of one of the oldest stock agencies into one of the newest. The most endangered segments of the Archive are now stored at minus four degrees Centigrade, conditions which, in conservation terms, "stop time." Thus immune to degradation, stock can fast-forward into digital multimedia and a bright future.

Put under a magnifier at the turn of the next century, what will the history of stock photography look like? Practical as well as philosophical, Bettmann conjectured, "Maybe in fifty years no one will be able to read — then the collection will be more valuable than ever." In a sense, this is already true: images are no longer "read" in the same way they were fifty or a hundred years ago, and this new literacy is arguably the result of re-reading and re-valuing the stock photograph.

---

below left: Barbara Kruger: *Untitled (It's a Small World But Not If You Have to Clean It),* 1990. Courtesy Mary Boone Gallery and the Museum of Contemporary Art, Los Angeles. Purchased with funds provided by the National Endowment for the Arts, a Federal agency, and Douglas S. Cramer.

below right: One more example of the "magnifying glass in front of the eye" genre. Otto Bettmann in 1988. Photo Michael O'Connor.

EXPLOSION
SARAH PICKERING

Atrocities have always occured during conflicts, yet in recent times combat training has become more and more realistic in order to psychologically prepare security forces for the worst. One result of this is the rapid expansion over the last five years of what are known as simulation pyrotechnics. Police and soldiers who have grown up playing computer games and seeing ever more spectacular special effects in films are simultaneously disconnected from and situated closer to the "real." The photographs reproduced here, which depict pyrotechnic explosions used by British police and military instructors to intensify the sense of drama and tension in training exercises, are part of a series taken at test sites in the English countryside where the bursts of light, flames, sparks, and smoke sit incongruously in the rural environment.

With names like "Artillery," "Groundburst," and "Napalm," the pyrotechnics evoke not only violent and destructive events from wars and conflicts, but also the dramatic re-enactments of such events familiar from feature films or war documentaries. Witnesses to extreme situations often describe what they saw as being "like a film," and modern filmmakers use CGI and special effects to conjure the most realistic possible disasters to entertain viewers. Whether real or artificial, we enjoy looking at explosions and, as an artist, I'm of course fascinated by their visual seductiveness. But I'm also interested in the forms of violence explosions represent, in our relationship to them, and in identifying the imaginative references they instantiate.

By using photography to record a simulated or imagined scene, I am creating a document that is already a departure from reality. Moreover, most of the photographs in this series were in fact taken during manufacturers' demonstrations for military and police shopping trips rather than during training itself—in this sense, the images represent artificial instances of artificial explosions, packaged here as "product." Both cataloguing and decontextualizing the explosions they depict, these photographs permanently suspend them in a tranquil and contemplative moment. The image of a past event hovers between "then," "now," and "what might be"; what should be a decisive moment is confounded.

opposite: *Groundburst No. 1*, 2004.

overleaf left: *Landmine*, 2005.

overleaf right: *Artillery*, 2005.

following pages: *Fireburst*, 2004.

You have
reached the
page on which
this book's
previous owner
decided to
give up.

You have
reached the
page on which
this book's
previous owner
decided to
give up.

PLACE THESE BOOKMARKS IN
BOOKS YOU WILL ABANDON

INSECURITY

NATIONAL INSECURITY

JEFFREY KASTNER

*I cordially concur with you in the prayer, that by God's
blessing this undertaking may conduce to the welfare of
my people, and to the common interests of the human race,
by encouraging the arts of peace and industry, strengthening
the bonds of union among the nations of the earth, and promoting a friendly and honourable rivalry in the useful exercise
of the faculties which have been conferred by a beneficent
Providence for the good and the happiness of mankind.*

    —From Queen Victoria's remarks at the opening of the
Great Exhibition of Works of Industry of All Nations, 1 May
1851

Delivered on a fine spring afternoon before an audience of
some 25,000, Victoria's brief inaugural oration for the Great
Exhibition marked the official opening of one of the grandest
and most ambitious peacetime endeavors of the nineteenth
century, and what was to become a watershed event in the
history of the burgeoning modern age. Over the next five
months, more than six million visitors would pass along the
soaring *allées* of Joseph Paxton's Crystal Palace—a sunlit
citadel of iron and glass erected over twenty-one
acres of London's Hyde Park—to view over 100,000

55

displays of artistic, commercial, scientific, and mechanical
achievement submitted by some 14,000 exhibitors from
Britain and her colonies, from continental Europe, and from
the United States. The first "world's fair" for a world then
becoming aware of its increasingly global character, the
Great Exhibition was foremost a prideful celebration of the
British Empire's cultural and industrial superiority. Yet even
as it served to physicalize the host nation's longstanding
preeminence on the world stage, the exposition also offered
early glimpses of its denouement. It enacted the "friendly
and honourable rivalry" between Britain and her economic
competitors in a broadly public context, as spectacle and
even a kind of entertainment, and with the real (if generally
thought to be unlikely) risk that she might be judged by that
public to be inferior to her upstart rivals for technological
and economic dominance.

    Accounts of the day do not record whether Alfred
Charles Hobbs was among the crowd assembled for the
Queen's dedication speech, but the young American locksmith would no doubt have heard in Victoria's words an
invitation to just the kind of challenge he had hoped to
find on his first trip abroad. Hobbs had come to London

above: The United States Court at the Crystal Palace. From *Dickinson's Comprehensive Pictures of the Great Exhibition of 1851.*

as a representative of the New York firm of Day & Newell, which was exhibiting as part of the exposition's American department. (Located in a prominent spot at the far western end of the building's central nave, the US display was an elaborate affair that featured, among other things, a life-sized section of Nathaniel Rider's new suspension truss bridge, a twelve-foot-high ziggurat fashioned from Charles Goodyear's vulcanized India rubber, and, to serenade visitors, a grand pipe organ draped with an American flag and surmounted by an enormous sculpture of a bald eagle.) For his part, Hobbs had brought with him a more modest, if no less extraordinary artifact: his boss Robert Newell's celebrated Parautoptic lock, a piece of machinery designed to compete with, and surpass, the security devices available at the time in Britain, generally agreed to be the finest in the world. Hobbs's plan was not only to promote the benefits of Newell's lock, but to do so by publicly demonstrating the insufficiency of its competitors. As it turned out, his method for accomplishing this goal became one of the most talked-about subplots in the story of the Great Exhibition.

• • •

Public excitement over the Exhibition did not abate following its grand debut and the major London newspapers dutifully covered the comings-and-goings in Hyde Park on a regular basis, and in exacting detail—announcing various daily events associated with the fair; recording the opinions of important personages; noting the arrival of visitors from abroad; and even cataloguing the contents of the Crystal Palace lost-and-found ("3 umbrella cases, 4 rings, 8 fans, 1 silver watch and guard, 1 operaglass, 2 toothpicks, 1 thimble…"). Four months into the show, the 7 September 1851 edition of the *News of the World* still devoted nearly 5,000 words to the news from Crystal Palace, trumpeting everything from the visit of "1000 workmen from Sunderland … accompanied by the Mayor of that town," to the arrival of an expedition of "Piedmontese artisans" come to inspect the "wonders of the Crystal Palace," and sneeringly reporting the opening of several "packages of articles … recently arrived from India" the contents of which, "being of the rudest possible manufacture, are extremely interesting as illustrating the state of society among the hill tribes in the province of Bhangalhore."

Near the top of the day's digest was an item headed "The Success of the American Lockpicker," regarding the contentious activities of none other than Mr. A. C. Hobbs of New York:

The lock controversy continues a subject of great interest at the Crystal Palace, and, indeed, is now become of general importance. We believed before the Exhibition opened that we had the best locks in the world, and among us Bramah and Chubb were reckoned quite as impregnable as Gibraltar—more so, indeed, for the key to the Mediterranean was taken by us, but none among us could penetrate into the locks and shoot the bolts of these masters. The mechanical spirit, however, is never at rest, and if it is lulled into a false state of listlessness in one branch of industry, and in one part of the world, elsewhere it springs up suddenly to admonish and reproach us with our supineness. Our descendents on the other side of the water are every now and then administering to the mother country a wholesome filial lesson upon this very text, and recently they have been "rubbing us up" with a severity which perhaps we merited for sneering at their shortcomings in the Exhibition.

That a controversy over locks would have "become of general importance" in Victorian England was more than a fluke—the mid-nineteenth century was a renaissance moment for the development of locking devices as an emerging middle class, increasingly congregated in population-dense urban areas, sought more efficient and reliable means to secure their homes and effects. In a sense, the issue of personal safekeeping was a microcosm of larger political concerns about security as well—a nation like Britain that had used its superior ingenuity to acquire vast wealth also had to be able to effectively protect it.

Though the first wooden pin locks (in which upright pegs on a toothbrush-like key lifted a set of matching pins on a simple bolt attached to the door) had appeared as early as 3000 BC in Egypt, it was the Romans who began to use metal for lock-making, and who introduced the concept of the "warded" lock—situated around the keyhole on the interior of the lock, a series of elaborate projections, or "wards," required a given key face to have a set of matching slots in order to turn freely within the housing. Pin locks and warding patterns dominated lock design up through the end of the eighteenth century, when predominantly English inventors like Robert Barron began to experiment with more complicated multiple-action tumbler locks; these used an advanced system of levers that had to be raised in their slots by the user's key to exactly the right level for their bolts to be released.

The names Bramah and Chubb hardly needed further introduction for the readers of the *News*—Jeremiah Chubb of Portsmouth, England, and Joseph Bramah of London were the Empire's two most eminent lockmakers. Chubb had gained fame in 1818 for the "Detector" lock that he devised with his brother and partner, Charles, which incorporated an ingenious spring device that grabbed any tumbler lifted too high (as by a false key or lockpicker's implement) and held it in place, simultaneously rendering the lock inoperable and preserving evidence of tampering. Meanwhile, Bramah, a successful engineer who in 1778 had patented the first flush toilet—featuring the float and valve system still used today—had turned his attention to lockmaking and with his assistant Henry Maudslay (a great engineer in his own right, whose pioneering work with machine tools was invaluable to his mentor's work) devised an altogether different sort of device. It was circular, and featured a small tubular key whose end was incised with a series of longitudinal slots that, when inserted into the lock, depressed a configuration of slides to a set correct depth to release the bolt. The eighteen-slider lock Bramah patented in 1787 was calculated to have more than 470 million possible permutations and was widely considered unpickable. Indeed, in 1801, Bramah made a public challenge to advertise his handiwork's impregnability, placing in the window of his shop at 124 Piccadilly a barrel-shaped padlock version of his patent lock, made specially by Maudslay and bearing the legend: *The Artist who can make an Instrument that will pick or Open this Lock, shall Receive 200 Guineas The Moment it is produced.*

As it happened, such an artist was now in their midst. Working to promote Newell's Parautoptic lock (so called because its design, which featured a kind of shutter around the keyhole, preventing inspection of the lock's interior by any would-be picker), Hobbs decided on a dramatic gesture, first boldly announcing one day to a group of scientific men gathered at the Crystal Palace that even the very finest British locks were eminently pickable—to prove his point, he produced one of Chubb's famous Detector locks and, in only a few minutes, picked it on the spot. As the story of Hobbs's conquest of the Chubb lock circulated, doubts were voiced by critics who were not present at the demonstration. Undeterred, the American issued a formal invitation to Messrs. Chubb, writing a letter on 21 July to inform the great lockmakers that he was to again pick one of their locks, this time in the presence of several important and impartial judges, including a former Secretary to the Board of Trade. A letter, issued the following day and signed by the eminences, made the results a matter of public record:

We the undersigned hereby certify that we attended, with the permission of Mr. Bell, of No. 34 Great George-street, Westminster, an invitation sent to us by A. C. Hobbs, of the City of New York, to witness an attempt to open a lock throwing three bolts and having six tumblers, affixed to the iron door of a strong-room or vault, built for the depository of valuable papers, and formerly occupied by the agents of the South-Eastern Railway; that we severally witnessed the operation, which Mr. Hobbs commenced at 35 minutes past 11 o'clock A.M., and opened the lock within 25 minutes. Mr. Hobbs having been requested to lock it again with his instruments, accomplished it in the short space of 7 minutes, without the slightest injury to the lock or door. We minutely examined the lock and door (having previously had the assurance of Mr. Bell that the keys had never been accessible to Mr. Hobbs, he having had permission to examine the keyhole only). We found a plate on the back of the door with the following inscription: "Chubb's New Patent (No. 261,461), St. Paul's Churchyard, London, Maker to Her Majesty."

Hobbs had used a series of specially-designed tools and small weights to undo what Chubb's advertisements called the "perfect security" of his lock in less than a half-hour, and the ease of his feat sent shockwaves through the British locksmithing community. No one from Chubb's firm had accepted Hobbs's invitation to attend the dem-

onstration, but the British lockmaker eventually accepted Hobbs's success, announcing that his locks would in future be updated and improved to prevent the methods Hobbs employed. And even as Hobbs was picking Chubb's lock, he had already set his next and greatest test, the defeat of Bramah's famous challenge lock, in motion. A committee of learned men was organized to supervise the arrangements and the lock was removed from its half-century-long perch in the Piccadilly window and taken to an upstairs room at Bramah's shop (which was now operated by his sons as Bramah & Co., Joseph having died in 1814), where it was sealed within a kind of wooden box so that only the keyhole was accessible. The room was given over to Hobbs's exclusive use and the American was allowed thirty days to complete his task. Work began on 24 July and, after being suspended for several weeks during a procedural disagreement, resumed on 16 August. On 23 August, Hobbs called in the committee to announce he had broken the challenge lock, and in several demonstrations over the next few days, repeatedly picked and restored Maudslay and Bramah's device in the presence of witnesses. In all, it took him fifty-one hours, spread over sixteen days, to accomplish his goal.[1]

After a great deal of disputation about the condition of the lock, the American's methods, and the precise terms of the challenge—much of it played out in the pages of daily newspapers like the *Observer*, which published both panicked letters from a banking community who had seen the vulnerabilities of their security publicly exposed and the rationalizations of the lockmakers trying to defend their now suspect products—a panel of arbitrators appointed to settle the affair finally ruled in favor of Hobbs. And so in early September, Bramah & Co. grudgingly paid the American £210 (the equivalent of 200 guineas). Yet the lock controversy had not yet quite played itself out. The week after Hobbs was paid, a certain Mr. Garbutt—a respected locksmith who had been responsible for the locks at the Crystal Palace cashier stations—announced that he would attempt to defeat the Newell Parautoptic lock, which like the Bramah had also been made available for public challenge at Crystal Palace.

The Newell lock was removed to a private home at No. 20 Knightsbridge, where it was secured within a wooden box like the one that had enclosed the Bramah lock the month before. At the end of the thirty days Garbutt had been allotted, he returned the lock, having failed to open it. (Trying to pick the Newell lock had by this point become something of a sport, as British engineers sought to restore some sense of national pride. Indeed in early 1852, following a presentation of a paper by Hobbs at the Royal Society of Arts, it was claimed by an audience member that the Parautoptic lock had in fact been picked by a London locksmith. The newspapers began circulating the rumor until Hobbs went public with the full story, eventually acknowledged by the locksmith who had supposedly defeated the Newell device, that he had in fact simply taken an impression of the key and copied it. This copy, wrote Hobbs in the *Observer* with not a little bit of sarcasm, was, not surprisingly, "found to lock and unlock the lock as readily as the original key.")

• • •

By the spring of 1852, the lock controversy had finally begun to ebb. In due course, the Jury Reports of the Great Exhibition were issued. Functioning in effect as the final scorecards for the "honourable rivalry" that had played out in the various departments of the Exhibition, these reports were prepared by prominent judges; Berlioz, for example, wrote the assessment of the musical instrument competition. Much to everyone's surprise, the jury on locks declared itself "not prepared to offer an opinion … on the comparative security afforded by the various locks" that had come before it. Of this opinion, a leading magazine of the day observed, "The jury seems to have consisted of the only persons in England who did not hear of the famous 'lock controversy' of last year; for one can hardly imagine that, if they had heard of a matter of so much consequence to the subject they were appointed to investigate, they would have altogether abstained from saying anything about it."

Yet by then all the rhetoric was of increasingly little consequence. The Bramah and Chubb companies continued to thrive in their businesses with newly improved technologies inspired by Hobbs's handiwork. Both firms are today still mainstays of the British security industry—Chubb is a multinational manufacturer of safes and surveillance devices, and Bramah, which still maintains a shop in central London, is primarily a maker of specialty locks for use in high-end furniture and residential design applications. Meanwhile, Hobbs took his prize money and instead of returning to New York and his bosses at Day & Newell, decided to stay in London, patenting his own lock, based on the design of the Parautoptic, and opening Hobbs & Co. at Cheapside in the heart of the City of London's banking district.

Hobbs remained in London for nearly a decade before returning to the US in 1860, where he worked as an engineer and designer for the Howe Sewing Machine Company and later at the Remington Arms Company. There is no record of Hobbs's involvement in lockmaking after his return. In any event, new talents had by then begun to emerge in the field, including Linus Yale, who as a young locksmith in upstate New York—far from the bright lights of the Great Exhibition—had picked the Day & Newell lock, it was said, using only a wooden stick. Hobbs's firm, which he sold but which retained his celebrated name, continued to operate for over ninety years at its original location in the City of London, and in 1954 was itself acquired—by the Chubb Group.

1 While the challenge lock itself had reportedly never been broken, Hobbs acknowledges in his accounts of the "lock controversy" that this was not in fact the first time someone had picked a Bramah lock. In 1817, an employee of the Bramah firm by the name of Russell apparently devised a means of picking his boss's locks and even took out advertisements touting his services to owners of Bramah locks who had lost their keys. See A. C. Hobbs, *Construction of Locks and Safes* [1868], ed. Charles Tomlinson (Bath, England: Kinghsmead Reprints, 1970).

READY FOR INSPECTION: AN INTERVIEW WITH VALENTIN GROEBNER

DAVID SERLIN

In spring 2006, National Public Radio reported that over the past few years the agency responsible for issuing passports in Iraq has been flooded by requests from Sunni Muslims who have wanted to change their surnames. The rise in murders and other violent acts committed against Sunnis has apparently encouraged thousands to take on new identities and thus identify themselves in entirely new ways in the Iraqi national register. Since many Sunnis can trace their ancestral names back to the seventh century, some might be less willing than others to sacrifice cultural heritage for the purposes of survival. But the story also speaks poignantly to the shifting relationship between one's personal identity and one's passport, which, in the current political climate, has never been more dramatic as aggressive measures to secure borders, register citizens, and limit travel are seen by some as the only solution to achieving global security.

In his forthcoming book, *In the Matter of the Person: Identification, Dissimulation, and Surveillance in the Middle Ages and the Renaissance* (Zone Books), Valentin Groebner, a professor of history at the University of Lucerne, Switzerland, argues that the emergence of the passport and the creation of bureaus for tracking individuals is far older than most people, and most historians, have previously recognized. Indeed, Groebner demonstrates that the social and political significance of the passport can be traced back hundreds of years to the practice of amassing enormous amounts of data about individuals and building vast agencies to manage and protect them. In arguing for the medieval origins of networks of registration and surveillance, Groebner's work challenges those who believe that the Kafkaesque tracking of individuals is something inaugurated by the modern era.

David Serlin spoke to Groebner by phone in May 2006.

How did you become interested in the history of the passport, which is not an object that we usually associate with the Middle Ages?

At some point I realized I had no idea what the history of the passport was, and there were no histories on the subject that went back further than the nineteenth century. My starting point was wondering how, before the age of photography and modern techniques of bureaucratic registration, people described themselves and were described by others who had never seen them. Think of the familiar situation in which you are going to meet someone you don't know in a crowded area, such as a bus station or an airport. Someone might describe the person's hairstyle or clothing, while others use film actors as a point of comparison: "He looks a little bit like Woody Allen, only with a big beard."

I had discovered in previous archival research that, in the past, people often described others by their clothing rather than the categories that we're familiar

with now. Some people disguised themselves simply by putting on a different coat, which is a strange idea to us. But, to my knowledge, there was no mention of eye color before the eighteenth century. Europeans typically described each other using a variety of skin colors, ranging from "yellowish" and "red" to "brown" and "black." "White" was used as an extreme skin color; echoing literary models from Antiquity, medieval and Renaissance writers reserved it for women or for huge, effeminate barbarians from extreme northern regions.

Prior to writing about passports, I had written a book that included a long chapter on the notion of the "invisible enemy," the enemy who is already within the city walls. They are invisible insofar as you do not know who they are, and the crucial thing is to identify them through the secret sign that marks them as conspirators. So I wanted to figure out when the first "Wanted" posters were put up, the first arrest warrants were issued, when passports were made compulsory, and what role images played in these techniques of identification.

At what point did the creation of passports as compulsory forms of identification become a means of identifying individuals with their country of origin?

Surprisingly, that appears very late. It's only after the second half of the 1850s that, in Europe, citizens were supposed to carry a passport issued by their home countries. For five hundred years, people were traveling with identity documents issued by any kind of sovereign. Practically all the British travelers to the continent from the seventeenth century onward equipped themselves with passports in Belgium and France because they were so much cheaper to buy there. The very strong nexus between the passport and nationality, the country or place of one's origin—which is in itself a modern term—is a product of combined developments of the late nineteenth century and the direct result of World War I.

The passport we carry in our pocket is itself a piece of frozen history that goes back much farther in time. It is quite medieval, because that is where its categories originated; even the material, such as paper, and the various stamps and seals that make it valid, are medieval in origin. The passport is, in fact, not really an artifact of the individual but an artifact of the issuing authority. I'm interested in the

opposite, clockwise from top:

1. A mid-sixteenth-century woodcut portrait of the child murderer Hans von Berstatt suggests the form of later "Wanted" posters.

2. Friedrich Nietzsche's passport from 1876.

3. Using this passport, Anselim Udezue successfully applied in 1998 for tourist visas for Austria, Germany, and Switzerland and subsequently toured the countries for nine months. It was not until his departure that a Swiss airport official noticed that "British Honduras," the state that had allegedly issued the passport, does not exist.

4. An 1888 advertisement for travel on the Orient Express. Note that no passport was needed between Paris and Constantinople.

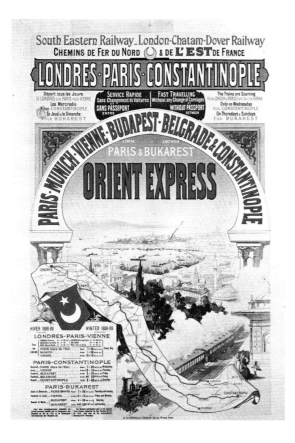

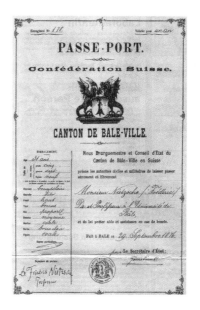

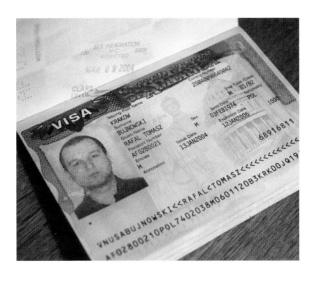

traces that authorities leave on paper rather than authorities' attempts to fix a person's allegedly unchangeable identity onto a piece of paper. From the beginning, these documents were about transforming people rather than fixing them, as we usually assume.

Would you then say that the creation of the "modern" passport takes place in the mid-nineteenth century because of the presumption that borders and territories need to be secured in a world governed by imperial powers?

Yes, but that sense of "national security" has a much longer prehistory. Of course, what is so striking is that the idea of securing your borders by registering all travelers and, if possible, all of your own subjects as well, is a fantasy of rule, a bureaucratic fiction. And that fiction is pretty old. It is the result of an adaptation of the Christian belief that God looks up everyone's deeds in his big book on the day of the final judgment. Authorities throughout Europe, from the sixteenth century onward, tried to establish a huge register in order to control the movements of their subjects, but it never worked out. The first attempts to establish such a system of complete registration, an all-seeing eye of the state, as it were, took place in the later sixteenth century. But it never worked, not even in the powerful Spanish-Habsburg empire. It just produced huge mountains of paper, which you can visit today in archives in Spain and Italy.

By focusing on the material stuff out of which an identity is made—that is, the seal, the paper, and the signature—it is obvious that the physical components that make a document valid are products of reproduction technology. The king's seal, or the city's stamp, is valid because it is the same on every document.

That's what gives it its authority.

Exactly. It's not the name on my passport that makes the document valid, but the categories of authentication, created through formal bureaucratic procedures that the document must bear, that make it truly valid. It was clear from the very beginning that the state's ability to produce an authentic document lies in its application of signs of authenticity to a document. Then, every technically able person was tempted to copy the reproductive signs and use them for their own purposes. That's why forged passports appeared only a few years after passports were made compulsory.

But long before the official passport, in the second half of the sixteenth century, a new figure appeared on the scene in Europe: the impostor, someone who has accumulated many impressive, personal, official documents to show that he is a rich merchant or Count So-and-So, except that all of these impressive documents are forged. The practices of forged identification always mirror those of the official normative documents that are introduced in order to survey, control, and register people on the move. What is so fascinating is that everyone knows what these official documents are supposed to look like.

These seem to be instances in which people did not create counterfeits based on a real person but instead created identity documents for someone who didn't exist, as opposed to what we might in the contemporary moment call "identity theft."

Yes, I suppose that's true. The case of the impostor as someone who "takes the place of another person," which is the literal meaning of the word, was relatively rare in Renaissance Europe. There were a few famous medieval cases; several people who, after the death of Emperor Fredrick II, for example, appeared as the wonderfully returned emperor. More often than not, though, people invented brand-new identities for themselves with the help of seals and impressive identity documents. A number of these impostors had impressive political careers. For example, there was a Jewish merchant named David Reuveni, who appeared first in Venice in 1524 and then in Rome claiming to be the brother-in-law of a powerful Jewish king in the East. Reuveni claimed that this king would be able and willing to attack the Ottoman Empire from the east if only he had a bit of cash. They were close to equipping him with a great deal of money and artillery to subsidize this fictional ally against the Turks in the East. Reuveni very nearly made it, but he was busted and disappeared in the prisons after the Holy Inquisition.

In practice, the huge registers built up from the sixteenth century onward did not serve as a real means to identify people. Pre-modern identification procedures relied on much more efficient means: informers, secret individuals who were good at finding people through informal techniques. It's like that character in Quentin Tarantino's film *Jackie Brown* who, when asked, "How did you find him?" replies simply, "It's my job to find people." These people have existed for a very long time. We have good information on these informers. Some worked part-time, others were fully employed by ruling princes or councils in many medieval cities, including Venice, which was infamous for its official spies and plainclothes informers. In addition, Florence had an entire system of official "post-boxes" installed specifically for informal notes on the secret denunciation of other citizens. People were invited to drop information on others into these boxes. This was an officially accepted practice.

It sounds like the Stasi in East Germany.

Well, in the fifteenth century, neither Florence nor Venice was a particularly fun place to live. But the system was not so much one of registering people through written

opposite: In 2004, Polish artist Rafal Bujnowski painted a portrait of himself and submitted a photograph of the painting in lieu of the usual black-and-white photograph required for applications for US visas. The staff at the US embassy was fooled and granted him a visa featuring his painted likeness, which he promptly used to enter the US where he took flying lessons over New York City airspace.

information. The much more efficient way was through denunciation, through secret official informers who kept an eye on people and helped to build an atmosphere in which you were never sure for whom the person at the next table, listening to your conversation, was working. That type of insecurity is a classic feature of pre-modern rule.

I suppose we are not that terribly modern in our ways of controlling the population. I can't help but feel that though we fear the all-seeing eye of the state upon us, be it through closed-circuit cameras, telephone calls, email exchanges, or through our genetic fingerprints, the techniques of surveillance have not greatly changed.

One of the most efficient techniques of control is creating an atmosphere in which you can never be sure if your official documents are valid or not. The very logic of compulsory registration is that you bring the person that is being controlled into a state of temporary insecurity in which he or she does not know the categories under which his or her passport or ID card is scrutinized. I have the feeling that the introduction of new passports and new devices of identification is creating situations of control in which you never can be sure if your passport is still valid, if your chip is OK, or if someone has tampered with your magnetic strip. You cannot ever be sure if your papers are good enough. Citizens of wealthy nations aren't accustomed to this because they safely assume that their traveling documents are first class. But anyone who carries a Mexican or Nigerian passport can probably tell a different story.

In what ways have the formal categories used in identification documents to describe people changed over the past few hundred years?

The use of distinguishing signs or marks in physical descriptions is very old, but it is still used in a lot of European passports. It clearly goes back to recording the scars and tattoos with which people were marked in order to be distinguishable. Our own skin is a piece of selective memory. What was registered as a distinguishing mark is in itself an interesting problem. Any analysis of the categories used to describe people in the past necessarily brings forward how mobile and flexible these categories were. Should freckles, for example, be considered distinguishing marks?

I'm sorry to say that, from a historical point of view, the new field of biometrics—the gathering of behavioral or physiological data about an individual—may well follow the way of its forerunners. It will be doomed because it will pile up so much information about the actual encoding, registering, and collecting apparatuses that the biometric data itself will become secondary. The process of collecting and ordering huge masses of data is more energy-consuming than those who build the registration apparatuses realize. The accumulation of biometric data will fall victim to the same entropy as the huge piles of paperwork in the archives of King Philip of Spain who, at the end of the sixteenth century, wanted positively to establish the identities of everyone emigrating to the New World in order to prevent

the offspring of Jews, Arabs, convicted heretics, runaway priests, and debtors from wandering across the Atlantic to start a new life. But that is what they did. All data run the risk of turning into a bureaucratic fantasy in which the already stored information is used to provide the categories of authenticity for new information.

Bureaucracies also need to collect data in order to justify their existence.

Yes. And in order to justify the validity of the data they have already collected. That is what happened in poor King Philip's archive; all those who left for the New World had applied with false documents. At some point a scribe in the Spanish court realized that they had tens of thousands of personal files, but the documents within these files had been forged. I'm not saying that all the biometric data will end up as forgery, but instead that there has been a tendency for huge collections of data to form into quasi-autonomous fantasies of a world in which everything registered is institutional.

So would you argue that the relationship between official identification and one's personal identity is something that well predates the modern era?

Well, to be honest, the word *identity* gives me a headache. As a term, it's rather problematic since it has at least three profoundly different uses or meanings. *Identitas*, a medieval word, refers to the Holy Trinity and to a very complicated theological debate about the sameness of very different principles within the trinity. *Identity* stands, simultaneously, for my own definition of myself in the first person—"I am X," as it were. But it is also used to label and denominate someone else—"You are X," which is quite a different meaning. Lastly, *identity* is used to describe a person's adherence to a group, a collective. These three distinct meanings magically blend into one when we use the term indiscriminately. It's a noun trick. So from the very beginning the term *identitas* already referred to reproduction, to doubling, to the proliferation of something within different media. It does not refer to an individualistic or essential principle but, rather, to the contrary. The more polemical passages in my book are about insisting that we replace the concept of identity with the process of identification, which involves multiple protagonists. Identity itself has no protagonists; it is something that can be conjured up from the ground. It is more a kind of cloud than a notion one can work with.

I must confess that, despite being a historian who works on the fifteenth and sixteenth centuries, the way I look at my material is always informed by the world I'm living in. We like to pretend that pre-modern peoples were simple individuals with simple identities who did not have to grapple with any of the problems that we attribute to modernity. But we have an obligation to treat the material we find in the archives in an intellectually responsible manner and not separate it from the sharp edges of modernity or a pre-modern lost world.

INTRUSION MOBILE
DAVID MILES

MATERIALS NEEDED

craft knife or scalpel, scissors, (invisible) thread, glue,
length of wire or thin dowel (approx. 20 cm), pin, hook

DIRECTIONS

1. Cut out the three elements (tip: remove inner spaces before
   cutting out whole piece). Use a pin to pierce holes in white
   spots for threading.

2. Lay the three elements and the
   wire support on a flat surface
   in their respective positions
   and distances away from each
   other (see the thumbnail on
   the front of this page). Make
   sure the sleeping man is in the
   center. Cut lengths of thread
   and connect elements to the
   support. A simple knot will
   suffice.

3. Attach another thread to the centre of the support
   for hanging. Once suspended, the positions of the
   elements can be adjusted to get the right balance,
   and then fixed into position with a touch of glue.

By looking at these complex forms of identification, it seems as if what you're trying to do in your book is challenge the fantasy that pre-modern peoples were somehow more "authentic" than those in the Renaissance and modern eras.

What I focus on is the degree to which people were able to imagine their own transformation, because identity papers are something that transforms us. When we are described and registered, we are also being transformed, and not just metaphorically speaking. Physical descriptions of people who have been conscripted for military service, or who were captured and sold as slaves, constitute some of the oldest registers we have. These people are transformed by being identified and described, in the most material sense of the word.

Since I was trained as an art historian and had learned about the "discovery" of subjectivity in Renaissance Italy, it was a revelation to discover that medieval people didn't believe that a portrait looked exactly like the person it was rendering. The portrait was always already understood as a mask, something artfully fabricated that might only have represented the secret, inner aura of the individual depicted in the portrait. So the fantasy of primordial authenticity and identity in the happy pre-modern world is simply of no analytical value whatsoever. It might be appealing, but it doesn't help us explain anything.

To what extent was your interest in the processes of identification for medieval and Renaissance peoples shaped by living in a post-9/11 world?

Well, the current political climate certainly has influenced the way I've thought about identification, but I wrote the first sketch of this book in the late summer of 1999. In January 2001, I conducted a long interview in the headquarters of the Swiss federal police with a group of specialists responsible for designing the then-new, forgery-proof Swiss passport. The specialists explained to me that they were ready for the first time to include a chip integrated with the passport holder's biometric data. After September 11, all of the research on biometric data, which had been initiated by credit card companies, became justified by the new terrorist threat. But all the technology was there beforehand.

When I asked why this was necessary, they explained it with the story of a woman from Kenya who was going to marry a Swiss man. She traveled from Mombassa to Zurich in order to get a new, authentic, original Swiss passport. After she received the passport, she put it in an envelope and sent it to her sister in Mombassa, who was roughly the same height and age as the woman. The sister then would be able to enter Switzerland unhindered because her passport would be considered authentic and valid. The Swiss police called this an example of the impostor problem and the reason why they wanted all passports to carry biometric data.

It is telling that the threatening image of the invisible outsider is used to justify allegedly powerful devices for registering and controlling all citizens in order

to sort out good ones from the bad. These are stories that sound familiar because we have heard them for nearly five hundred years. Of course, this is a European perspective because we have had stricter obligations to be registered by the state and carry passports and identity cards for the last hundred years. But understood within the context of the history of the passport, the biometric model is merely a new version of the centuries-old gap between the person and the document that has to re-present, re-produce, and re-naturalize the citizen. Our submission to the unknown workings of bureaucracy is a very old principle, but it is the principle under which passports and identification procedures have operated since the sixteenth and seventeenth centuries.

This interview is published as part of *Cabinet*'s contribution to *documenta 12 magazines*, a collective worldwide editorial project linking over seventy print and on-line periodicals, as well as other media. See <www.documenta.de> for more information on documenta 12 and this project.

PAPERWORK
BENJAMIN KAFKA

In 1802, two journalists, Étienne and Martainville, published a history of the French theater since the beginning of the Revolution. One of its footnotes told a strange story. During the final months of the Terror, following a performance of a stage adaptation of Richardson's *Pamela, or Virtue Rewarded* perceived as counter-revolutionary, the Committee of Public Safety had decided to send the members of the Comédie Française to be judged by the Revolutionary Tribunal. The crowds had gathered to watch these celebrities escorted from the prison to the courtroom for a sentence that would surely be severe. But they never showed up. The trial had been postponed because the paperwork was missing. Étienne and Martainville reported that the actors and actresses had been rescued by "a simple employee of the Committee of Public Safety named Charles-Hippolyte Labussière, who, risking his life, removed all the documents." Not only had he removed these documents, he had destroyed them "in the most ingenious way." Labussière "went to the baths, soaked all of the documents until they were almost reduced to paste, and then launched them, in small pellets, through the window of the bathing room into the river." The Terror came to an end before new papers could be drawn up. The note concluded by claiming that the members of the Comédie Française had not been the only ones rescued by this clerk: "More than two hundred people owe him his existence."[1]

Interest was piqued. Within months of the book's publication, a letter appeared in the widely read *Journal des Débats* elaborating on the footnote. The letter was signed "J.C.T.," initials that probably belonged to Joseph-Charles Trouvé, former editor of the quasi-official newspaper *Le Moniteur Universel,* later a diplomat and prefect—in other words, a man of considerable credibility.[2] After reading the footnote, he had sought out Labussière in person. Trouvé was now writing this account of his meeting "as a monument to the cruelty of men and the humanity of a simple individual to whom we owe the preservation of more than twelve hundred victims condemned to perish for their virtues, their wealth, or their talents." His version of the story is worth quoting at length:

Charles-Hippolyte Labussière entered into the Committee of Public Safety's Prisoners Bureau as a copy clerk three and a half months before 9 Thermidor. This Prisoners Bureau provided information concerning prisoners throughout the Republic and served as a depository for documents delivered to the Popular Commission, by order of the Committee of Public Safety, so that they could be handed over to the Revolutionary Tribunal. Labussière was the clerk to whom the documents came last, to be numbered and registered. Every day, at two in the afternoon, he would give them to a member of the Popular Commission, who was instructed to take them from his hands without giving him a receipt. Forty-eight hours later the detainees were judged, which is to say, sent to the scaffold.

Labussière, from the very first moment of his entry into the Prisoners Bureau, had already conceived of his project to

above: Engraving of Robespierre laid out on the table at the Committee of Public Safety, waiting to be taken to the guillotine on the morning of 10 Thermidor.

use his position in favor of as many victims as he could save. Every day he had twenty to twenty-five documents to give to the commission. He began first by removing the Sénéchal family, Madame Leprestre de Château-Giron and her two daughters. During the first six days he was content to hide the documents. However, since the volume began to grow too large, and since he could neither take them out during the day, nor keep them hidden, he imagined a way to make them disappear during the night. He would thus return to the Committee of Public Safety at one o'clock in the morning, while the members of the committee were deliberating. He would climb up to his office, go to his hiding-place, take the documents, soak them in a bucket of water, and make six or seven balls out of the paste, which he would put in his pockets. Towards six o'clock in the morning he would go to the baths, where he would soak these same balls of paper some more, since they had already hardened because of the extreme heat (it was the early days of Messidor). He would subdivide them into smaller balls which he would then toss into the Seine through the window of his bath.

This letter built towards the night of 27 June when Labussière discovered the documents concerning the trial of the members of the Comédie Française. Narrowly evading detection, he succeeded in destroying their dossiers and saving French theater. The letter concluded by mentioning that after the coup of Thermidor, which brought an end to the Terror, Labussière had continued to work to liberate political prisoners.[3]

Thanks to this footnote, Labussière was on his way to celebrity. In 1802 his portrait appeared in the Salon. And in the spring of 1803 the Comédie Française, after several false starts, staged a performance of *Hamlet* for his benefit at the Théâtre de la Porte Saint-Martin—the first performance of the play in France in nearly twenty years.[4] The performance was attended by First Consul Napoleon Bonaparte himself, in the company of Josephine, another prisoner during the Terror whom he was credited with having rescued. A letter of gratitude from Labussière appeared in the theatrical paper *Le Courrier des Spectacles*. This appears to be the only version of his story written in his own words:

During this bloody period, horrible to remember, I had the pleasure of saving many victims from the revolutionary axe, at the risk of my life. How happy I would have been if this had not also involved the cruel necessity of risking the lives, more than once, of my comrades in the Prisoners Bureau, where I was hired as a copy clerk. I used a stratagem as simple as it was bizarre! I avow that, without their courageous humanity, all of my efforts would have been useless. They unofficially closed their eyes to my thefts and, through their silence, associated themselves with the glories and dangers of my enterprises. The tigers that drank the blood of men, although seized by fear and suspicion, were not careful enough to suspect me. My neglected exterior and my frank and joking tone gave me an air of simplicity that made me seem unimportant in their eyes. I dared to be human in an era where humanity was a crime.

In the letter Labussière claimed to have rescued exactly 1,153 people from the guillotine. He had then returned to private life, all but forgotten, until Étienne and Martainville rescued him from obscurity.[5]

An authorized biography appeared in 1804. Written by an enterprising lawyer, *Charles, ou Mémoires historiques de M. de la Bussière, ex-employé au Comité de Salut Public* recounted its subject's life in four small volumes of treacly prose. He had been born in 1768 to an ennobled family protected at court by the famously ill-fated Princesse de Lamballe. Inspired by a love of the theater, he had eventually moved to Paris to take part in small productions. The Revolution provided him with a new opportunity for acting out. He would disrupt section meetings by introducing absurd motions. He would attract large audiences in the gardens of the Palais-Royal by denouncing the latest conspiracy to steal something from him—once the suspense had built sufficiently he would reveal the thing to have been only his handkerchief. These anecdotes always concluded with his narrow escape from the humiliated sans-culotte mobs.

It is not entirely clear from the biography how Labussière ended up working for the Committee of Public Safety. It merely states that his friends, concerned that he was endangering himself with his antics, arranged for the position because they felt that it would be safer for him there. Labussière was assigned to the Prisoners Bureau, under the direction of Fabien Pillet, a man of letters who, like Labussière, was opposed to the terrorist regime. It was Pillet who suggested to Labussière that "the occupations of the employees, far from harming the unfortunate detainees, can help them. This office is nothing, and yet it is a lot." Nothing because, to all appearances, it was simply a brief stop for a small number of the documents circulating within the revolutionary government. A lot because "we can sometimes suspend the voracious activities of the Revolutionary Tribunal by working slowly and multiplying obstructions. At the slightest pretext we can delay, as long as possible, the transfer of documents to the Popular Commission. This way we give the detainees time to have their relatives or friends intervene by bribing committee members who are the absolute masters over the lives of men."[6]

Labussière was put in charge of evidentiary documents. Once registered, these documents were handed over to the agent of the Popular Commission who arrived each day at two o'clock. The agent neither counted the documents nor provided a receipt. His sloppiness provided Labussière with the opportunity he needed. He hid his first documents shortly after entering the offices of the Committee of Public Safety. He soon removed more, and then more still, locking them all in his desk drawer. At first he acted cautiously, worried that the agent would notice that files were missing. But after realizing just how little order there was in the paperwork, he settled on the scheme that would make him famous. Flashing his entry card to the guards in front, he would return to the Tuileries late at night, climb to his office in the Pavillion de Flore, and take the documents he had hidden in his desk during normal business hours. He would soak them in a bucket of water kept in the offices to chill the wine; form the paste into small pellets that he could hide in his pockets; transport the pellets to the public baths to be soaked and shredded some more; finally toss the papers through the window into the river. "These ingenious methods were the only ones possible during these times of *rigorous surveillance*," the memoirs explain, "because *burning the documents* was impractical, especially during the heat of summer, when fire would seem unnecessary or suspect; because *transporting the documents* in their natural state would have been imprudent, given their volume and the guards' strict orders." As for the final shredding of the documents in the public baths, it was necessary because the larger pellets quickly dried out in the summer heat and might float to the top of the Seine, thus exposing the sabotage. By mid-June, Labussière had disposed of 800 files.[7] By the end of June, he had rescued the French theater. And by the end of July, it was over. Labussière resigned from the Committee of Public Safety after making sure to "efface even the slightest traces of his hard work."[8]

• • •

The most reliable account of Labussière's later years was provided by Fabien Pillet, his friend, supervisor, and accomplice. Writing the entry for Michaud's *Biographie Universelle* in the 1840s, Pillet recounted how the benefit performance at the Théâtre de la Porte Saint-Martin had raised 1,400 francs for the former clerk. "But, unable to economize, Labussière soon dissipated this sum, and, despite the secret aid of the Empress Josephine, via the hands of Madame de la Rouchefoucauld, he fell into a state of extreme misery. Following a violent attack of paralysis, his intellectual faculties became so deranged that the police were forced to keep him locked up in a madhouse, where he died soon after, entirely forgotten even by those for whom he most risked his life."[9] (Pillet himself went on to become a noted arts critic, dying in 1855. Of his own adventures, the *Michaud* mentions only that he had "the good fortune to pass unnoticed during the reign of terror.")[10]

But the story did not end with the life of its protagonist. It would be novelized, dramatized, filmed, and even, during the bicentennial celebrations, made-for-television. In 1891, a play about Labussière, Victorien Sardou's *Thermidor*, sparked riots for its allegedly anti-republican sentiments. The riots, in turn, sparked an editorial in the *New York Times*, which expressed bewilderment that Parisians had become so agitated over so simple a story. "The play seems to go no further than an implication that the guillotine sometimes makes mistakes," they wrote. "A similar dramatic presentation of the case against lynch law would be received without hostility in a Western mining camp and might be attended and enjoyed by the members of the latest vigilance committee."[11] Alas, the French could muster no such tolerance. Banned in France, the play traveled abroad, including to New York, where it sold well despite tepid reviews. The ban was finally lifted in 1894; a restaurant on the

Boulevard Saint-Denis celebrated re-opening night by placing on its menu a new culinary creation, lobster Thermidor.

The controversy generated by Sardou's play would last through the *fin-de-siècle*, engaging some of France's most prominent historians. Of the various twentieth-century versions of the Labussière story, one still stands out. In 1927, Abel Gance released his bio-epic *Napoléon*, whose importance in France is perhaps best compared to that of D. W. Griffith's *Birth of a Nation* in the United States. The scene featuring Labussière begins with a shot of papers stacked to the ceiling inside the Committee of Public Safety. A man suspended from a rope moves up and down the shelves, retrieving dossiers. An official passes them to a clerk and orders him to hurry: there must be 300 heads a day. The camera then pulls back to reveal a hectic, cluttered office. The clerk scurries back to his desk and sets down to work. He comes across a dossier with the name Josephine de Beauharnais. The camera closes in as he bites into it, spastically chewing, swallowing, digesting. The clerk next to him watches in wonder and then follows his example, soon devouring the dossier for Napoleon Bonaparte. "Happily, Labussière watches over them, this strange character who, out of humanity, became a thief of dossiers," an intertitle tells us. "Not a thief, but a *chewer*, risking his life at every instant to save the lives of unknowns."[12] Through this act of papyrophagy, the republic is sacrificed, the empire born.

1 Charles-Guillaume Étienne and Alphonse-Louis-Dieudonné Martainville, *Histoire du théâtre français depuis le commencement de la révolution jusqu'à la réunion générale*, 4 vols. (Paris: Chez Barba, Year X/1802), vol. 3, pp. 146-48.

2 This attribution is suggested by Arthur Pougin, *La Comédie Française et La Révolution: Scènes, Récits et Notices* (Paris: Gaultier, Magnier & Cie, 1902), p. 148.

3 *Journal des débats et loix du pouvoir legislatif et des actes du gouvernement* (5 Messidor, Year X), pp. 2-3.

4 *Le Courrier des Spectacles*, 24 Germinal, Year XI (14 April 1803).

5 Ibid.

6 Nicolas-Julien Liénart, *Charles, ou Mémoires historiques de M. de la Bussière, ex-employé au Comité de Salut Public, servant de suite à l'Histoire de la Révolution française, avec des notes sur les événemens extraordinaires arrivés sous le règne des Décemvirs, rédigés par M. Liénart*. 4 vols. (Paris, 1804), vol. 4, pp. 95–96.

7 Ibid., vol. 3, pp. 99–110.

8 Ibid., vol. 3, p. 132.

9 Louis Gabriel Michaud, ed., *Biographie universelle, ancienne et moderne*, 2nd ed., 45 vols. (Paris: Vivès, 1880); s.v. *Labussière (Charles-Hippolyte)*.

10 Michaud, *Biographie universelle*, s.v. *Pillet (Fabien)*.

11 Untitled editorial, *The New York Times*, 28 January 1891, p. 4.

12 An illustrated and annotated version of the script, including the director's notes, can be found in Abel Gance, *Napoleon. Épopée cinégraphique en cinq époques. Première époque. Bonaparte* (Paris: Jacques Bertoin, 1991).

opposite: stills from Abel Gance's *Napoléon*, 1927.

WEAPONS OF MASS REDUCTION

GAGE McWEENY

In the mid-1990s, United Nations peacekeeping forces in Somalia were equipped with a new type of weapon to help troops contend with urban environments in which militia fighters often mixed with unarmed civilians. The new weapon was comprised of a tank to be worn like a backpack with a hose running from the tank to a gun with a nozzle on it. Rather than shooting bullets, this new gun shot streams of sticky chemical foam that would almost instantly immobilize someone with a heap of viscous bubbles, pinning him to the ground Spiderman-style without any lasting harm. The sticky foam gun was to be a new weapon of less destruction, a means of crowd control whose conceptual precursor was less rubber bullets and more Legion of Superheroes. Deployed to Somalia but never actually used on people by UN troops, the sticky foam gun nevertheless kind of stuck, as a vision of future warfare with less lethality.

After decades of life under nuclear threat in the Cold War, the sticky foam gun at once emblematized a messier world in which humanitarian intervention, peacekeeping, and war were becoming increasingly blurred, and also seemed like a hokey throwback to Cold War science fiction utopianism. The image of soldiers blasting away with soapy-looking foam instead of using riot batons was almost quaint. With the foam stored in silver cylinders mounted on backpacks, the sticky foam gun had a kind of campy James Bond jetpack look to it, like something from the future, if your present is, say, 1958.

But in this future, the weapons have been engineered to be less lethal to the same degree that they are used for engagement with crowds of non-combatants; that is, non-lethal weapons are made for use on what used to be called civilians before non-state conflicts turned everyone into either combatants or non-combatants. While the sticky foam gun has a kind of endearing utopian quality to it, a sense that peacekeeping operations might best be handled by Spiderman, the quaintness of sticky foam also may turn out to be part of a charm offensive that softens us up to this new kind of war.

• • •

At least since Gustave Le Bon's 1895 *The Crowd: A Study of the Popular Mind*, a work that popularized and distorted a host of nineteenth-century social theory and mass psychology into a vision of the fearsome arrival of "the era of the crowd," there's been a steady industry in efforts to understand and to control the crowd. Le Bon predicted a coming world of mass, if not quite mob, rule, with the crowd possessing a supreme social and political force. Now, the United States Army has its own new guide to crowd control, FM 3-19.15 *Civil Disturbance Operations*, published in April 2005. The army manual reads a bit like Le Bon's own field guide, but with all the apocalyptic rhetoric carefully drained from it by the strictly-business language of military writing. The manual is at pains to point out to its users that the right to assemble is protected by the United States constitution, and it catalogues various outmoded, prejudiced understandings of how crowds behave handed down by Le Bon and his heirs, while putting forward its own more scientific taxonomy of the crowd. The Army manual is a compelling read, and through it one can learn all about the four different types of crowds (Casual, Sighting, Agitated, Mob-Like), as well as the various techniques and sophisticated forms of weaponry developed in recent years by the army to deal with them.

The military has at its disposal what Le Bon, not to say the Marx brothers, could never have dreamed of for the purposes of crowd control: sticky foam. Or, at least for a short time in the mid-1990s they did. When shot from a gun with a nozzle on it, sticky foam expands to thirty times its stored volume, and can glue a person to a surface with its super adhesiveness or just render them too gooey to move. In pictures, getting sticky-foamed looks roughly akin to being attacked by an enormous bag of marshmallows. In one photograph showing a demonstration of sticky foam on a US soldier, General Anthony Zinni, who oversaw the deployment of sticky foam guns in peacekeeping operations in Somalia, can be seen laughing as the soldier lies on the ground covered in foam, looking as much like dessert as subdued. With the appearance of a shaving cream fight gone bad, sticky foam has none of the publicity fallout of rubber bullets, which can kill if used at close range, and doesn't result in the ominous and utterly broadcastable images of crowds of civilians being teargassed. After a person has been immobilized, the sticky foam, which is made out of rubbers, resins, oils, and flame retardants, can be removed, eventually, with hard scrubbing and baby oil.

Originally developed in the late 1970s by Sandia National Laboratories in New Mexico as a last line of defense to protect nuclear facilities from intruders, sticky foam is part of a new range of non-lethal weapons, weapons whose primary aim is to incapacitate while minimizing fatalities and permanent injuries. Non-lethals are the Marvel comics of military technology, as if a bunch of tech types were given the opportunity to develop the various superpowers of superheroes and supervillains into actual weapons. The new line of non-lethal weapons employs technologies far more exotic than bullets in an effort to do less damage. Low-frequency acoustical weapons, for example, can cause incapacitating nausea via sound waves. Something called the Active Denial System emits a quick burst of painful electro-magnetic energy, causing lots of pain, but no lasting injury. Other new technologies include the Mobility Denial System, in which slippery fluid is sprayed from a backpack onto the ground, making the terrain impassable; sponge grenades; and self-destructing bullets that break up into painful, but not fatal, rubber balls before impact.

What's driving all this non-lethality is a sense, beginning in the early 1990s, that the United States would need

opposite: A sticky foam test. Courtesy Sandia National Laboratories.

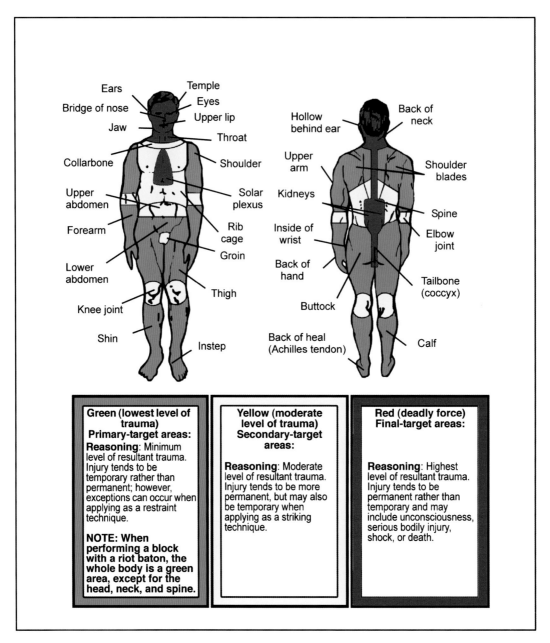

Figure 4-4. Escalation of Trauma Chart

to adapt to increasing engagements in non-state warfare and peacekeeping operations. Some in the military pushed for technology that might better allow troops to deal with situations involving crowded, urban environments in which armed combatants mixed in with civilian populations. Such situations are referred to as "non-traditional battlefields," and are part of what people in the business call Military Operations in Urban Terrain, or MOUT. As any image of US military involvement in Haiti, Kosovo, Somalia, or Iraq in the past decade or so shows, there's been a lot more MOUT lately. And where there's MOUT, there's the increased possibility of non-combatant casualties. Non-lethal weapons advocates argue that this is the future face of war, and non-lethal weapons allow soldiers to take more appropriate, and more politically acceptable, actions in crowded urban areas when firing a gun with bullets or beanbags, or shooting tear-gas canisters, are not the only options.

In 1996, the United States Department of Defense issued a directive for the creation of the Joint Non-Lethal Weapons Program (JNLWP) to be overseen by the US Marines. (One of the features of US military writing is acronym-philia, which seems to come from twin but conflicting impulses toward brief, efficient communication and the endless expansion of agencies, protocols, directorates, etc., whose names are comprised of multiple words. The JNLWP website has a link to its list of acronyms. I counted forty-five.) All kinds of debates about the nomenclature of not-death surround the technical reports on these weapons. For the non-lethalists, the weapons are designed to incapacitate temporarily, so "non" is the appropriate prefix for something whose intended purpose is not to kill. The less-than-lethalists argue that anything, even a marshmallow, can be lethal, given the right conditions, and so the weapons should properly be called "less-than-lethal" in order to reflect their specifically disabling qualities, but without making any promises about non-death. But for sheer macabre semantic pleasure, it's hard to beat "pre-lethal," a term used for technology that is meant to stun or temporarily incapacitate combatants long enough for them to then be killed with a follow-up strike. Of course, all technology is, strictly speaking, pre-lethal, including marshmallows, since we'll all die eventually.[1]

The JNLWP website contains plenty of photographs of American soldiers and weapons not being lethal. This non-, or less-than, lethality is transpiring for the most part among identifiably non-American, and basically identifiably Middle Eastern, people in the photos. Because the photographs are untitled and so generic in form and content, it's hard to tell if the pictures are from training exercises or if they document actual engagements. In one picture, a soldier in a military vehicle appears to be having a heated exchange with a crowd of civilians who are slightly below him; the soldier holds out one hand in an apparent effort to either calm or repel the people gathered around him. In another, a man in a kaftan is shown reading a newspaper at an outdoor café, politely ignoring an American soldier a few yards away in front of a Humvee, who seems

to be politely doing the same thing, albeit with a gun in his hand.

There are no captions to the photos identifying where or when they were taken, but of course, they all read as Iraq. The Cold War American sociologist Erving Goffman argues that such poses of polite indifference, what Goffman calls "civil inattention," are crucial to maintaining zones of privacy for individuals amidst the crowdedness of city life. In an anticipation of late-twentieth-century non-lethal weaponry, Goffman credits such acts with preventing urban social life from being "unbearably sticky," keeping us from innumerable unwanted social engagements with strangers on the street, or simply being swallowed up by the crowd. But, of course, daily life under peacekeeping, with restricted areas, curfews, checkpoints, and more, must be "unbearably sticky" for those who experience it. Under these conditions, sticky foam might be almost beside the point, or maybe just an apt, both cartoonish and real, intensification of what is already the point: mobility in MOUTs or under peacekeeping is restricted.

•   •   •

Once considered a joke by more hawk-ish types, non-lethal weapons are now a swiftly expanding industry, with military contractors evolving new technologies to accommodate the changing terrain of war. But these weapons also do a lot of much-needed psychic work in accommodating us to the future of a US military engaged in a series of protracted police or peacekeeping activities across the globe. If the weapons used in MOUT remind us of the powers wielded by superheroes, of 1950s technological utopianism, that little bit of campiness might be what makes us more able to live with superhero rhetoric about battles between Good and Evil. Sticky foam, with all its rich slapstick potential, is a non-lethal weapon that's hard not to love. And who wouldn't want to find some comfort or comic relief in such non-lethality after Abu Ghraib, amidst boobytraps, beheadings, and the rest of the horrors of post- (and pre-) invasion Iraq?

One can only dream of how history, film history, might have been different had Harpo Marx been among those first armed with a sticky foam gun. Or, more close to contemporary hand, and maybe more apt, Sandia National Laboratories need have looked no farther than Johnny Knoxville and the gang of masochistic Buster Keaton heirs he presides over in the film and television program *Jackass* for their sticky gun test subjects. (As it was, Sandia went, where else, but to Florida, and where else in Florida but to prisons, to test sticky guns as a crowd control tool for use on inmate populations). And one can only imagine, and in doing so no doubt still fall short of Knoxville's own talents for imagining, the varieties of self-inflicted humiliation and gross-out dares, the kinds of sticky foam field tests that he and his crew might have performed on themselves, free of charge. In fact, Knoxville and company may turn out to have

73

opposite: From "Civil Disturbance Operations," US Army Publication FM 3-19.15.

formulated a new genre for a new kind of wartime, something like Late-Imperial Slapstick. Laughing as Steve-o and the rest dare each other to snort wasabi through their noses, light bottle rockets out of their asses, and more, we're no less horrified when we then see photos of prisoners being tortured by US soldiers. But we're familiar already with the genre of the image, familiar enough with humiliation as filmable entertainment.

In 1997, Amnesty International reported on the use of electro-shock devices similar to Tasers, which deliver a 50,000-volt shock, as instruments of torture in more than fifty nations. With little regulation or oversight of the use or distribution of electro-shock weapons, their non-lethality is precisely the quality that makes them suitable for torture. What are the tools of torture, the stuff of Abu Ghraib and elsewhere, but the re-purposing of official or improvised technologies into methods of applying precise amounts of painful non-lethality? Called into being by the convergence of military action and policing or peacekeeping, non-lethals are becoming increasingly popular with police forces for domestic use as well. Watching a news feed of crowds getting non-lethaled in a conflict on the other side of the world is familiar enough now, but that familiarity may become tinged with the *unheimlich* as non-lethality at home and abroad become harder to distinguish.

• • •

Recently, sticky foam has had a Cold War comeback moment, with the Department of Energy reportedly reintroducing it back into its old role of safeguarding sensitive areas of nuclear facilities from terrorist attack. Stored under pressure in metal containers within the steel doors of nucle-

ar sites, sticky foam turns from liquid to solid upon exposure to air should someone attempt to break through the door. The attacker would be instantly coated with the stuff, slowing him down long enough for more responders to arrive.

In this new-old job, sticky foam acts as what security types call a "force multiplier"; in military terms, a factor or technology that increases the effectiveness of troops in combat. Sticky foam, ready to glom onto intruders at nuclear facilities, the argument goes, would allow the facility to increase security without having to hire more personnel. Having largely been retired from its use as a crowd control weapon in gun form (after Somalia, it was determined that the use of sticky foam in guns carried too great a risk of fatality from suffocation should the foam be sprayed on someone's mouth or nose), sticky foam technology is now getting its own turn to function something like a crowd, allowing security personnel to multiply their force from that of the relative few into that of the many. Since Spiderman's own super powers are the result of being bitten by a radioactive spider, there's a nice symmetry to his non-lethal weapons avatar, sticky foam, being back in action at nuclear plants.

Whether other non-lethal weapons will limit fatalities and collateral damage in war and peacekeeping operations is an open question, but given how horrifying non-lethality can be when it takes the form of torture, such weapons may turn out to be one of the central moral problems for the war against terror. The very cultural work they do in acclimating us to the notion of war with less lethality may be their most dangerous aspect.

1 For the true believers, non-lethal seems to have won the day. Retired Colonel John B. Alexander's very useful book *Future War: Non-Lethal Weapons in Twenty-First-Century Warfare* is a kind of layman's guide to, and polemic on behalf of, the centrality of non-lethal tactics and weaponry for future conflicts. The very fact that it's got both "non-lethal" and "Tom Clancy" on the cover page (Clancy wrote the foreword) would seem to settle the issue. It's an interesting book for its overview of non-lethal warfare technology, but also because it enjoys a kind of porous relationship between the reality-based world and the fictional worlds depicted in military- and technology-heavy books by people like Tom Clancy and Michael Crichton, both of whose novels are cited by *Future War*. Alexander often begins with possible terrorist scenarios, setting things up by saying, "Imagine this Hollywood script," and then goes on to show how that particular scene wouldn't be possible (read: not very dramatically satisfying) once, say, sticky foam was deployed to save the day. In a kind of pork-barrel politics of fiction writing, he thanks Tom Clancy in the acknowledgments for "including non-lethal weapons—where appropriate—in his books." Even in the fictional world of Tom Clancy, evidently, where and when to use non-lethals is a tough call to make, and it's a good thing Tom Clancy has the presence of mind to make those calls. In reading up on this stuff, one starts to suspect that a flexible border between the world we live in now, the lethal and often technologically very simple one of Improvised Explosive Devices, and the fictional, more advanced, less lethal one imagined as the Future, is one of the features of being a hardcore non-lethalist.

left: **Suds aplenty, courtesy of Sandia National Laboratories.**

EXPANSION, CONFRONTATION, CONTAINMENT: AN INTERVIEW WITH REVIEL NETZ

JEFFREY KASTNER & SINA NAJAFI

While many tools of war embody the violence for which they were intended in their very physical forms, few materials evoke the dangers and desperation of modern military conflict as vividly as barbed wire. Though some precursors were invented in France and the US in the 1860s, the history of barbed wire began in earnest in 1874, when an Illinois farmer named Joseph F. Glidden took out a series of US patents on his design for the material. Production in America's northern industrial centers grew rapidly in the late-nineteenth century as this "devil's rope," as it was colloquially called, became the preferred method of delimiting territory in the open spaces of the nation's Great Plains—270 tons were manufactured in the US in the year following Glidden's patent; by the end of the century, production had increased to some 135,000 tons a year. As the volume of barbed wire grew, its uses diversified—its extraordinary trajectory during the first half of the 1900s would see it spread from the cattle ranges of Texas to the world's battlefields, and eventually to the catastrophic precincts of the Soviet gulag and Nazi concentration camps.

In his recent book, *Barbed Wire: An Ecology of Modernity* (Wesleyan University Press, 2004), Reviel Netz, Professor at Stanford University, charts the evolution of barbed wire from its agricultural beginnings to its military and political apotheoses. A cost-effective, eminently uncomplicated, and remarkably successful instrument for the exercise of depersonalized control over large-scale space and movement—both of animals and of humans—barbed wire has a central role in modern history, writes Netz, "due to the simple and unchanging equation of flesh and iron." Ubiquitous at once as materiel and metaphor, barbed wire is for Netz a symbol for both the ingenuity, and the cruelty, of the modern age. Jeffrey Kastner and Sina Najafi spoke to Netz by phone at his office in Palo Alto, California.

Most of your research seems to involve the history of mathematics. How did you come to write about barbed wire?

I was living in England and was offered a job at Stanford, so I began reading about western American history. And at the same time I happened to be re-reading Solzhenitsyn. I was struck by the fact that barbed wire was invented in the American West—and it quickly became clear that to answer the question of how barbed wire made the transition from there to the Soviet gulag, one needed to understand global history, to understand biology, agriculture, the history of warfare, modern political history. I also had this realization that there is a vivid continuity between the violence that people mete out to animals and the violence that people mete out to other people—this was a fundamental *gestalt* shift for me, seeing history as being made of one piece, not humans and animals on one hand, and humans and humans on the other, but that we're all in it together in some sense.

Let's return to this original moment, to the invention of barbed wire. Although there were a few early patents taken out in France for something quite like barbed wire, such as the "metallic thorn" wire patented by Louis Jannin in 1865, the story of barbed wire is generally agreed to have begun in DeKalb, Illinois. It's 1873 and a farmer named Joseph Glidden goes to a county fair where he sees an invention being displayed by a local cattleman, Henry Rose.

Yes, Rose has a cow that tends to break through fences—he calls her "breachy"—and what he uses is a kind of collar with nails on it that he attaches in such a way that when the cow gets into tight spaces, the nails scratch against the skin and make it unpleasant for her. Rose realized that he could put the barbs on the fence itself—it wasn't a very sophisticated tool that he showed at the fair, basically just a piece of board with some nails on it. But Glidden's observation was that one could attach those barbs to a wire and this way could save on wood, because they didn't have much wood out on the plains and it was too expensive to import. This concept also grew out of the longstanding practice of planting hedges with sharp thorns that deterred animals from approaching them—again, this was something that people had tried to bring to the plains, but the distances were too great for hedges to be effective. So the need for a kind of fence in a place where wood was scarce, and for a thorny hedge where one could not be grown, both also coincide with the rise of industrialized iron production—and all this came together at that moment in the invention of barbed wire.

This is a watershed moment in many ways, particularly in the kinds of politics and economics of space that will be so central to the rise of modernity.

Absolutely. Barbed wire starts from the range experience with animals, where the cattle of the American West did actually "range" over an entire area. And they are gradually fenced in until the entire animal industry moves to a ranch model where animals are no longer fenced *out* of an agricultural field, but fenced *in* within an area defined for them. And this is a general historical trajectory we see in the uses of barbed wire in many aspects of modernity—that it starts out defining areas from which someone is to be excluded, until finally you remove the excluded one *into* his or her own reservation, so to speak, the excluded finally being limited to a very small space.

With the rise of new manufacturing technologies, barbed wire very quickly comes to be produced in the centers of American industrial production—indeed, it becomes one of the ways that the American West is secured as an outlet for the economies of the Northeast, which is where barbed wire is actually produced. This was also true for the cows themselves, of course, which would have been directly or indirectly controlled by loans coming out of the banking centers of the Northeast. So we can see an entire system of control developing: just as the cows are literally controlled by the barbed wire surrounding them, there is this more abstract system of control reaching out to the American West from the centers of capitalist power.

These themes are part of a kind of archeology of globalization, which is sometimes erroneously seen as a phenomenon of the 1990s. The history of globalization is in a sense as long as the history of the human race, but there is a central transition taking place in the middle of the nineteenth century, with the rise of the telegraph, the rise of the railroad, the rise of barbed wire: all tools that allow control over mass scale, away from the centers, which is the fundamental structure of globalization. At the time we called it imperialism, but now we call it globalization. We understand it better in these terms because imperialism is not the point, conquest is not the point—the point is control, the point is connectivity. This is what happens over the last century-and-a-half and barbed wire is a central tool, and a central metaphor, for this development.

In the early days of barbed wire, what was the rhetoric that its inventors used to promote their product?

You can see a very rapid transition in terms of rhetoric as soon as barbed wire makes its very quick and successful reach into wider areas. It starts out in a very limited, very specified domain—as a tool of the American West, the American plains. Texas is where it takes root, though it was, as you say, invented in Illinois. It first comes out of the ruggedness of the frontier experience, and there is an explicit rhetoric of violence and power around it—it's powerful, simple, it can exercise control—and it very quickly wins over the West and begins to be sold everywhere, on the Eastern seaboard and in Europe and its colonies. It's patented by Glidden in 1874, and by the late 1870s it's already a global phenomenon.

And now, because it's becoming so much more visible, the rhetoric around it changes. It's one thing to use it on the open plains, but another if you're going to put it in, say, Connecticut—people there actually debated it quite seriously at the time, and the legislature tried to stop its introduction into the state because people said it was too ugly, too dangerous, and it was going to harm animals. And so there the rhetoric became one of subtle control—it's only going to scratch the animals a little, just enough to control them. In fact, the two rhetorics still survive. There is, on the one hand, a fascination with barbed wire as a tool of explicit violence, and, on the other, the idea of barbed wire as a tool of progress that signifies ever subtler control of animals and better accommodation of humans and animals.

You've spoken about this rapid expansion of barbed wire across the globe within a decade of its invention. And only a decade after that, we see a rapid shift in its use, as well—a move from this agricultural and economic implementation to a confrontational, military one. And the signal moment of this in the history you sketch is the Boer War in the final years of the nineteenth century. Why is this an important moment?

The type of huge capitalist control of which only America in the late-nineteenth century is really capable creates a steep decline in price. Barbed wire is ultimately a very simple tool—nothing more than cut iron put together, the kind of thing where you can very quickly develop economies of scale and production. And while it isn't much in terms of total output—of course, machinery uses much more iron and steel—in terms of profit, it's one of the things that really drives the iron and steel industry, just because it's so easy to make. So barbed wire becomes very cheap by the end of the nineteenth century. This is important because it's now widely available and you can easily get large quantities of it, and so you can experiment with it. And such experiments occur in the Boer War in both the military and the civil realm.

The Boer War is a war between two entire cultures, between the British and the Boers of South Africa. The Boers tried to preserve their civilization, which had its own

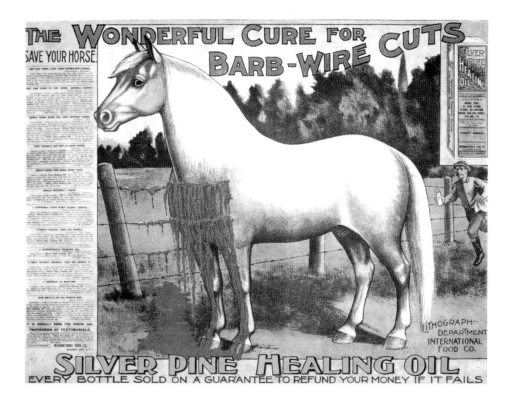

unpleasant aspects such as racism and xenophobia which one should not gloss over. But certainly they appear as the weak side in this confrontation, where essentially Britain tries to gain control over the gold of South Africa, naturally out of the hands of the Boers. And this confrontation very quickly becomes a confrontation with an entire nation and the Boers rise up in guerilla war against the British. On the one hand, you've got Boer men in the field, mounted on horses in small bands of sharpshooters, and quite efficiently attacking the British with classic guerilla warfare tactics. On the other hand, there are the women and children staying home and supplying the men on a clandestine basis. And the British did what armies fighting against guerilla forces usually end up doing—they fought the entire nation indiscriminately. The Boer villages are burnt down to remove the bases and the families become refugees and are removed to camps. The British want to give these sites a neutral name, so they call them "concentration camps," and this is how that term is introduced.

The Boers supply themselves by horse, the British by railroad—thus it turns out to be very important to gain and maintain control over the railroads. To do this, the British take to constructing long lines of fortified barbed wire along the rail system of South Africa. So curiously enough, just as the concentration camp is given its name, it is also constituted in the form we're familiar with in the twentieth century—the British need to set up quick structures to keep people in and they have this perfect material that's already on hand. And so you have barbed wire

settlements created for the first time, and called concentration camps for the first time, in the Boer War.

Now there are concentration camps for the civilian population and enormous barbed wire fortifications to protect the railroad and something funny is happening. Because the railroads crisscross the entire South African landscape, the outcome of protecting the system that way is that, in fact, it's not just fencing the Boers out of the railroads, it's also fencing the Boer warriors in within the pockets created by the pattern of the rails. And then they began what was called "the drive"—the British hunting the Boers exactly as the Boers themselves used to hunt animals, against barbed wire lines, with essentially columns of soldiers wiping out the guerilla forces from those quadrants created between the lines of barbed wire fortification.

And this dual role—in both civilian control and military strategy—continues to be refined in World War I.

Yes, and they will go hand in hand from this point forward. Barbed wire becomes the standard tool for the quick concentration of people at a time of war, starting with prisoners of war, but also with enemy populations that must be interned because there is a war and they might turn against you. At the same time, there is a growing realization that barbed wire is very effective in preventing soldiers from

above: Advertisement for Silver Pine Healing Oil, ca. 1880–1890. Animal injury constituted a major element in the early debates around barbed wire.

crossing the battlefield and is being used now together with trenches and with the evolving machine gun. This is something experimented with very extensively in the Russo-Japanese War of 1905 and, of course, this entire strategy comes to dominate Europe in World War I, where indeed barbed wire returned with a vengeance and came to define spaces in ways that are even more radical than in the American West. From now on, it's going to stay a fixture of Europe for the next thirty years—people are going to stop each other and intern each other using barbed wire.

When you write about the evolving uses of barbed wire in World War I, you also mention the development of the tank, which was in many respects a direct response to the use of this trio of obstacles—the barbed wire, the trench, and the machine gun. The tank also ironically came out of the same American rural, agricultural context as barbed wire, emerging from the technology of the farm tractor.

In North America, where you have mass production of agriculture, you need to think of new ways to control space in an economical way. And tractors were coming into use at the beginning of twentieth century as especially American agriculture had the need for more powerful tools to plow ever larger fields, where horses were no longer sufficient. The tractor becomes cheaper and cheaper to produce and eventually people realized they could adapt this farm tool that crosses any field, just as horses used to, to the battlefield, where the horse is now forbidden because the field has been strewn with material that was invented explicitly to prevent the movement of animals.

Was the barbed wire used in World War I essentially the same barbed wire that Glidden made? Or were there attempts to improve it along the way?

There are always different kinds of barbed wire and constant tinkering with it. The two main questions are how sharp and long the barbs are and what their density is. The sharper, longer, and denser they are, the more *vicious* they are, in the technical language of barbed wire design. You can follow a certain historical process. Barbed wire was invented as part of the violence of the American West; it's vicious because people needed a certain violence to control their animals. When cows become used to it, you don't need it to be as violent, because they're now afraid of it—after all, ranchers and farmers don't want to actually injure their animals—so barbed wire becomes less vicious as its use becomes more widespread. Then in World War I, there's the rapid transformation toward maximum viciousness again. The barbed wire used in the field for military purposes in World War I is the most vicious ever produced: very sharp, very long, and very, very dense. It's very different from the barbed wire that we're familiar with—it's really just one barb after another, there's nowhere to hold onto without barbs, and the soldiers keep complaining about getting cut while they're laying it out.

78

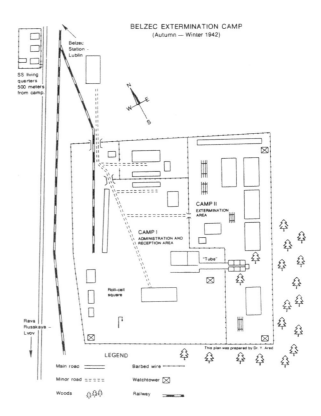

BELZEC EXTERMINATION CAMP
(Autumn — Winter 1942)

You note the standardization of barbed wire production and use during World War I. What happens in the years after the war?

Barbed wire essentially undergoes a transformation into a tool of political policy, in which the idea of containment we first see with civilian populations in the Boer War reaches its apotheosis. In Russia, it comes out of their prisoner-of-war policy. During war, things happen suddenly and you can't anticipate them—you have to improvise. And the prisoner-of-war problem then is how to improvise ways to deal with unanticipated groups of people. The Russians, among other nations, had a lot of prisoners-of-war, and so they put them in barbed wire concentration camps—it's a tool that you can easily put up and that had become a natural thing to do.

So in Russia, World War I evolves into a civil war. However there's a twist to it—in this war, the enemy is invisible in a sense. The enemy doesn't come from an enemy nation, it doesn't have a passport. This is a society, then, that always

above: Belzec, the first specially designated Nazi death camp, was gradually built from February 1942 onwards. Measuring only 265 yards by 275 yards, two rectangular areas were eventually carved out with the aid of barbed wire for accomodation and extermination. Reproduced from Yitzhak Arad, *Belzec, Sobibor, Treblinka: The Operation Reinhard Death Camps* (Indiana University Press, 1999).

opposite: A staged photograph depicting Nebraskan fence-cutters "taking the law into their own hands." There were frequent clashes between the proponents of open range and the advocates of barbed wire.

lives inside its paranoia of an enemy within, one that needs to be excluded: it lives with this exercise of looking out for the enemy, of reaching out for the enemy. And the war never ends: the mentality that was in place first in World War I and then in the civil war becomes part of the Soviet mentality. In the 1920s, even when the civil war is over, they're still talking of fronts, new battles, enemies. And when they decide to renew the war for Communism, together with war come prisoners, concentration camps, and barbed wire. So by the late 1920s, with the start of collectivization, the Soviet planners explicitly see the need to build up concentration camps. And these quickly become huge projects—by the early 1930s, there are already millions of Soviet people interned inside barbed wire.

And in World War II?

Barbed wire becomes simply ubiquitous. To give a poignant example: In 1939, when World War II started, the French have to do something about their potential enemy population, so they do the normal thing—they send people to barbed wire concentration camps. And who is this enemy population? It is refugees, primarily from Germany and Austria. And so in the fall of 1939, the French are involved in the paradoxical exercise of taking quite a few thousand Jews who fled Hitler and putting them in concentration camps. In the summer of 1940, these refugees remain in concentration camps, because they are still viewed as potential enemies

by their new occupiers, either by the Vichy or directly by the Germans. And then in 1942, those people are sent to Auschwitz to be killed there. You can follow an entire trajectory of people from the fall of 1939, Jewish refugees from Germany and France going through several camps over several years, until they reach the ultimate camp of Auschwitz, always within barbed wire yet within very different contexts.

Of course the Nazis, like the Russians, also have an internal enemy, one without a passport—although the Germans do actually stamp Jewish passports and eventually will stamp Jews themselves and, indeed, will brand them in the concentration camps, in another echo of the animal industry. But the Nazis need to get people out of a space, to remove people, and it must be understood that when you hear about schemes to send the Jews to Madagascar, etc., this is not just mad talk, this is not just a smokescreen. This is the way they think—in terms of exclusion, in terms of defining space. And this then, by the same logic we have seen elsewhere, leads to narrower and narrower spaces, until the natural conclusion arises in the Final Solution that this space of control and exclusion, always defined by barbed wire, must become a space of elimination.

This interview is published as part of *Cabinet*'s contribution to *documenta 12 magazines*, a collective worldwide editorial project linking over seventy print and on-line periodicals, as well as other media. See <www.documenta.de> for more information on documenta 12 and this project.

Below and pages 83, 84, and 86–87: Photos by Adam Broomberg and Oliver Chanarin, from their forthcoming book *Chicago* (SteidlMack). Given the international outcry that followed the April 2002 destruction of the center of the Jenin refugee camp, the IDF realized that it had to push its engineering corps to improve its "art of destruction," which had apparently spun out of control. As part of these efforts, two months after the attack on Jenin, in June 2002, the military started to build a series of urban warfare training sites and to upgrade existing ones. The mock-up town of Shizafon (pages 86–87), located in the Negev desert and hidden from view by mountains, reflects Israeli Orientalist fantasy. Another small mock-up town called Chicago (below and pages 83 and 84) and also located in the Negev, was upgraded into the world's largest fabricated Oriental city since the filming of *Ben-Hur*. In fact the "urban" history of Chicago has shadow-tracked much of the history of the military operations that have taken place in the Middle East, reflecting a series of changes in how Israel imagines its security. The core of Chicago was built as a small training site for IDF urban operations in Lebanon. It later expanded to accommodate the training of IDF special forces for their aborted operation to assassinate Saddam Hussein in Tiqrit. Chicago further expanded before the Iraq war to allow for heavy military vehicles and was used for training by the US Marines. In the summer of 2005, training for the evacuation of the Gaza settlements took place there, with actors playing settlers barricading themselves within their homes. Chicago now includes an area called the Kasbah (a historical-looking market area with narrow alleys), an urban outskirts, a refugee camp, a downtown area, and even an adjacent rural village. Before some special training sessions, the IDF invites a stage designer, usually employed at a Tel Aviv theater, to provide and organize the relevant props.

BETWEEN THE STRIATED AND THE SMOOTH
SHIMON NAVEH

The theater of our present wars is increasingly, if not exclusively, cities. This has driven militaries around the world to reflect on an emergent relationship between armed conflicts and the built environment. The urban environment is increasingly understood by military thinkers neither simply as the backdrop for conflict, nor as its mere consequence, but as a dynamic field locked in a feedback-based relationship with the diverse forces operating within it—the urban inhabitants, soldiers, guerrillas, journalists, and humanitarian agents. Because contemporary urban warfare plays itself out increasingly through the destruction, construction, reorganization, and subversion of space, architecture and planning become among the most important reference disciplines for military men.

According to geographer Stephen Graham, a vast, international "intellectual field" that he calls a "shadow world of military urban research institutes and training centers" has been established in the last decade in order to rethink military operations in urban terrain.[1] Its expanding network includes schools, urban research institutes, and training centers, as well as mechanisms for the exchange of knowledge between different militaries such as conferences, workshops, and joint training exercises. In their attempt to comprehend urban life, soldiers, who are the urban practitioners of today, take crash courses to master topics such as urban infrastructure, complex system analysis, structural stability, and building techniques; they appeal as well to a variety of theories and methodologies produced within contemporary civilian academia.[2] Indeed, the reading lists of contemporary military institutions include works from around 1968 (with a special emphasis on the writings of Deleuze, Guattari, Bataille, and Debord), as well as more contemporary writings on urbanism, psychology, cybernetics, and postcolonial and poststructuralist theory.[3] If writers claiming that the space for criticality has to some extent withered away in late twentieth-century capitalist culture are right, it surely seems to have found a place to flourish in the military. Furthermore, according to urban theorist Simon Marvin, the military-architectural "shadow world" is currently generating more intense and well-funded urban research programs than all university programs put together.[4] In no uncertain terms, education in the humanities—often believed to be the most powerful weapon *against* imperialism—is being appropriated as a powerful weapon *of* imperialism.

The practical and theoretical basis of urban warfare emerged from nineteenth-century colonialism, with French North Africa, in particular, seen as a laboratory for innovations in the field of governance and control. The French general Thomas Bugeaud wrote the first urban warfare manual—"La Guerre des Rues et des Maisons"—in 1849 (a chapter from this book is available at <www.cabinetmagazine.org/22/bugeaud.php>), a year after returning from Algiers, where he commanded the French

expeditionary force, and in response to the upheavals in Paris in 1848. In Algiers, Bugeaud brutally practiced "counter-insurgency" through the reshaping of the colonial cities and countryside by acts of destruction (razing villages and widening city roads) and construction (building markets, military bases, civilian settlements) to suit his needs of control. In his book, Bugeaud devised similar methods of repression through design—whether to be conducted through battle or in anticipation of it—in response to the class-based struggles of Industrial Revolution-era Paris.

The central "laboratory" for the development of contemporary urban operations roday is no doubt the occupied Palestinian territories. During the second Intifada (2000–), the attacks of the Israeli army on the Palestinian cities and refugee camps were studied in great detail by foreign militaries—especially the American and the British, as they prepared themselves for the occupation of Iraq—but also, significantly, by civilian planners as they sought to devise ways of protecting city centers from terror attacks.[5]

Shimon Naveh is a retired brigadier general, Israel's foremost philosopher-soldier-cum-urban-theorist, and director of what the Israel Defense Forces (IDF) calls the Operational Theory Research Institute. In the following text, he describes the meeting that preceded the 3 April 2002 attack on the refugee camps of Balata and the Old City of Nablus—an attack that killed more than eighty Palestinian civilians and combatants, and destroyed and damaged many of the city buildings. This attack, commanded by Aviv Kochavi, has become the most influential case study for military study of operations in urban terrain. The following text is based on transcripts of a command meeting that took place several days before the attack. It has been written by Naveh as an educational tool in the form of a short-story drama in order to be more accessible for soldiers who will read it in the Staff and Command School where he teaches.

It is important to note that, although based on and conducted through reshaping the battle-space, the intention in this attack was not to gain territory or control it, but to be able to locate the members of the Palestinian resistance, kill them, and leave. The horrific reality of these objectives is part of a general Israeli policy that seeks to disrupt Palestinian resistance through the assassinations of military and political activists. Such *necrotactics* would thus come to imply the reversal of the traditional aims of warfare. The military does not kill enemy soldiers as a means to obtain the strategic ground they occupy, but temporarily enters strategic ground in order to kill its enemies. Killing is not a by-product of military maneuver, but the very essence of the current Israeli campaign against Palestinian guerrilla and terror, and thus has become, in the absence of any legal process to support it, and since the definition of "immanent danger" is extended to all members of the resistance and their supporters, a systematic campaign of murder. It is mainly, but not exclusively, this logic of the attack on Nablus that would explain current calls for Kochavi, the "hero" of the following saga, to face a war-crime tribunal.[6]

—*Eyal Weizman*

1 I have witnessed some of these conferences. In January 2003, Stephen Graham gave me half of his £ 1,000 ticket to attend the second day of the Annual "Urban Warfare Conference" organized by a Security Institute in London called SMI. This was a surreal event where military personnel, arms dealers, and academics from NATO, the UK, the US, and Israel as well as representative of the RAND corporation, exchanged practical views on urban military operations and essential equipment within the conference hall and over dinner. On another such military conference organized in 2002 by the Faculty of Geography at Haifa University see Stephen Graham, "Remember Fallujah: Demonizing Place, Constructing Atrocity," *Society and Space*, 2005, vol. 23, pp. 1–10.

2 A publication prepared under the direction of the former Chairman of the US Joint Chiefs of Staff, Lieutenant General John P. Abizaid, and published in September 2002 under the title "Doctrine for Joint Urban Operations," (available at <www.dtic.mil/doctrine/jpoperationsseriespubs.htm>) divides cities, like much else in the military, into three composite parts, termed the "urban triad". The first part includes physical structure—buildings and roads—the hardware of a city. "Design by destruction" implies the shaping of the battle space to suit operational objectives. The second component is urban infrastructure. In modern cities with functioning, hierarchical networks of infrastructure, obtaining strategic control of, or being able to activate and deactivate key networks, such as roads, power supplies, water, and communication, may be more effective than controlling an urban space by military presence. The third component is the urban population, which can be manipulated by Psychological Operations to act according to military interests.

3 One of the reading lists of the Operational Theory Research Institute contained the following titles (amongst many other): Gregory Bateson, *Steps to An Ecology of Mind*, Beatriz Colomina (guest editor), *Architecture Production*, Gilles Deleuze and Felix Guattari, *A Thousand Plateaus* and *What is Philosophy?*, Clifford Geertz, *After the Fact–Two Countries, Four Decades, One Anthropologist*, Catherine Ingraham, *Architecture and the Burdens of Linearity*, Jean-François Lyotard, *The Post-Modern Condition*, Marshall McLuhan and Quentin Fiore, *The Medium is the Massage*, W. J. T. Mitchell, *The Logic of Architecture*, Lewis Mumford, *The Myth of the Machine*, Ilya Prigogine, *Exploring Complexity*, John Rajchman, *The Deleuze Connections*, Bernard Tschumi, *Questions on Space*, and Paul Virilio, *The Lost Dimension*.

4 Simon Marvin, "Military Urban Research Programs: Normalising the Remote Control of Cities," paper delivered to the conference, "Cities as Strategic Sites: Militarisation Anti-Globalization & Warfare," Centre for Sustainable Urban and Regional Futures, Manchester, November 2002.

5 Hundreds of US Marine Corps officers have trained in Israel over the last years in urban warfare and targeted assassinations, and in what the military crudely calls "population management"—a term inclusive enough to incorporate everything from an extended policy of curfews and blockades to the management of the civil affairs of the occupied by an occupying army. See "U.S. Marines Use Israeli Tactics in Falluja and Baghdad," *Middle East Newsline*, 10 November 2004, vol. 6, no. 418; Justin Huggler, "Israelis trained US troops in Jenin-style Urban Warfare," *The Independent*, 29 March 2003; Yagil Henkin, "The Best Way Into Baghdad," *The New York Times*, 3 April 2003. See minutes from a meeting titled "US-Israeli Seminar on Military Innovation and Experimentation" where US military staff is said to be impressed with the quality of the Israeli delegation that included, on this occasion, Shimon Naveh. The US officer taking notes concluded the minutes of the discussion thus: "I cannot do justice to his ideas, I simply did not get all he had to say. They seemed a lot like brainstorming, evaluating universals for relevance (discarding those considered not relevant, or out of date), then reexamining the problem from a new frame of reference. I AM SURE THEY WOULD HAVE A TITLE FOR MY NARROW INABILITY TO UNDERSTAND. [emphasis in original] But another outcome is Dr. Gold (with Andy Marshall's blessing) is seeking an opportunity for them to return to the JAWP and give us the Readers Digest version of their IDF course. You should plan to attend, when it comes." <http://www.belisarius.com/modern_business_strategy/moore/mie_1_us-israeli_seminar.doc>, 18 May 2006.

6 Kochavi captured the attention of the media in February 2006 when the chief legal advisor to the IDF recommended that he not make a planned trip to a UK-based military academy for fear that he could be prosecuted for war crimes in Britain. Also see Neve Gordon, "Aviv Kochavi, How Did You Become a War Criminal?" <www.counterpunch.org/nevegordon1.html>, 8 April 2002.

The large grey-metallic aerial photo lay on the huge oval wooden table like a deceased dinosaur thrown out of its habitat by some primary force. Marked by a white label carrying the name Raphidiya, the upper left portion of the Kodak paper was splashed with a turbid stain of sour military coffee. The air in the frosty fluorescent-lit room was heavy with the odors of human sweat, boot polish, rifle oil, and cigarette smoke. Fifteen pairs of somber eyes concentrated on a dark tight square on the lower right marked by the label "Balata," meaning "plate."

Aviv (meaning "spring" in Hebrew, a rather strange name for a professional soldier), commander of 35 Para Brigade, cut the heavy silence with his quiet voice: "There is reliable information indicating that a group of armed insurgents has moved recently from Nablus with the intention of establishing an operational base in Balata refugee camp. … Central Command wants us to go in and uproot them!"

"Oooh," mumbled Amir, the tall, fair-haired commander of Battalion X. "You mean go in and seize a built-up area? We have not done that since 1982, and, as I recollect, we were not particularly successful on that occasion…"

"Well," responded Aviv thoughtfully, "first, there is always a first time in war, as you all know. Second, this operation is not about seizing space, it is about preempting a problem, a ticking bomb! Third, our real problem is not attempting something that we have not done before, but rather freeing ourselves from a myth that has been debilitating the performance of state militaries for the last two centuries. Moreover, what worries me even further is the fact that at the moment no existing military doctrine can provide us with a relevant conceptual reference. Thus, we have to invent a new pattern of action, while relying exclusively on our own experience."

"What do you have in your bag for us, Shai, you magician?" said Aviv addressing the Brigade S-2 [intelligence staff officer]. "Well" said Shai, "Mainly bad news; intelligence in this operation is beyond your worst dreams."

"Stop frightening us! There is a serious fight ahead of us, and we are short of morale anyway," grinned Aviv.

Shai: "We know that between 80 to 200 armed insurgents from various organizations left Nablus in recent weeks and established themselves in the Balata refugee camp. We don't know their exact whereabouts, we don't know their command organization, and we don't know their operational deployment. All we know is that they have established an urban guerrilla base within the camp enclosure."

"High command must be joking," sarcastically mumbled Roni, the decent, thoughtful commander of Battalion Y. "This contradicts everything we have been trained to do."

"Wait!" said Shai, "We have not gotten to the worst yet. Remember how we rationalized the insurgents' attraction to the urban environment? It provides them with a natural base for operations against conventional forces; it affords them a human shield, which they cunningly manipulate; it is a natural hideout; an unlimited logistical base; a stage for spectacular brutality; a medium for disappearance. Built-up areas are reflectors of the regulars' [regular army forces']

form, and deflectors of the irregulars' [guerrilla forces']. Observing the addiction of state armies to conventional geometry and mechanistic order, on the one hand, and their phobia of casualties, on the other, subversive entities developed the doctrine that no conventional military will commit itself to a serious fight in the urban jungle. And, if the worst comes, the regulars will either succumb to the town's striation, or be defeated by the counterproductive effect of their mass firepower. In fact, we ourselves have become victims of this mythological argument." Becoming suddenly embarrassed by his over-enthusiasm, Shai took a deep breath trying to cool down.

Exploiting the lull in Shai's flow of speech, David, Z Battalion commander, fired a nervous question into the room: "So why should a group of insurgents bother to leave the haven of a big town and lock themselves in a remote, wretched ghetto like Balata?"

"Well," said Shai, "I think they either want to test our nerves, or pull us into a bitter fight. Whatever option materializes, they think they will humiliate the IDF in the same manner Hezbollah did two years ago. If we refrain from a fight, Abu Amar's [Arafat] warriors and a community of untouchables gain a psychological victory. If we accept their invitation, they believe they will embarrass us by bleeding us white. Since they expect us to come in the old style—mechanized formations in cohesive lines and massed columns conforming to the geometrical order of the street network pattern—Balata, almost deterministically, becomes a Palestinian Stalingrad."

"Without being drawn into over-detailed speculation," continued Shai, "by attempting to establish a *laager*, I think they have been fortifying all entries to the camp, mining and booby-trapping streets and alleys, both against soldiers and vehicles, and gathering whatever fighting materials and resources they can. In other words, by transforming Balata into a castle, they have set the stage for a fighting spectacle in which they expect us, when attacking the enclave, to obey the spatial logic that is most convenient for them." A heavy silence overcame the audience.

"There is nothing I like more than a hopeless situation," uttered Roni ironically, the rest bursting into laughter.

"Actually, things are not that bad," said Aviv. "In fact, together with Tamir, commander of the 1st Infantry Brigade, I have worked out an idea that you may find relevant to the setting of the problem we have been hovering around. Our impression is that some unique cognitive aspects that have not been observed by the insurgents can be manipulated in a manner that distorts both their thinking processes and their modes of behavior. In other words, if we apply critical thinking, we may have a chance of formalizing the subversive."

Aviv rose up from his seat and approached the drawing board. "Look," he proceeded, "the insurgents tend to misperceive their tactical (individual or team level of action) inconspicuousness (disappearance) as operational (system or organizational level of functioning) imperceptibility (absence). Their transition to Balata is about fighting, and fighting is about physical as well as conceptual cohesion. Moreover, this transition from a state of divergence (disappearance through non-contiguous deployment within a big town or city) to a state of convergence implies both a reframing of the relations between mass and space, and a reexamination of the tension between disappearance and fighting. Once they attach themselves to an enclave, tactically we may not see them until we engage them in a mechanical sense. Yet, operationally, unconsciously, they converge with the overall form (layout) of the enclave. So, we may not know the exact whereabouts of every fighting element, yet we have rationalized their institutional logic and conceptualized their systemic or operational form. That is not bad for a start, do you agree with me?"

"Thus," continued Aviv, "since the boundaries of the enclave reflect their operational form, we can design a complex fractal pattern of maneuver that will disguise our form from them, impose chaotic conditions on their cognitive process, and deconstruct or de-structure their operational form. In other words, striate what they discern as smooth."

"What worries me now are the following issues: First, how do we free ourselves tactically from the tyranny imposed on us by their tactical striation, which is to say, how do we avoid the traditional dictate of channeling our fighting units into linear streets and alleys? Second, since we cannot afford to utilize our most advantageous resource—firepower—and thus warfighting will be on even terms with our subversive rivals, how do we manage to disguise our tactical form from them while forcing them to disclose theirs?"

"Well, Aviv," interrupted Amir, "while you've been developing your operational ideas, we've been deliberating on the pragmatics of warfighting. If you are ready to compromise on some principled sensitivities and overcome some tactical mind-sets, I think we have a revolutionary solution to the tactical problems you indicated. Two of my boys, a platoon commander and his sergeant, both from kibutz Giva'at Haiim, think that once we penetrate an urban enclave, we should conduct our tactical movements through the houses or buildings and not around them. Our experiments with this new mode have taught us two things. First, we need to organize ourselves for breaking through walls and moving through the houses of individual families. Second, navigation and orientation must be thought through institutionally."

For the second time, silence settled in the room. Aviv, in his usual manner of discursive command, asked each of the participants for his individual opinion on Amir's concept.

Following the remarks of Nimrod, the commander of the reconnaissance company and the last of the participants to speak, Aviv turned to Shmulik, the brigade S-3 [operations officer], and summed up his thoughts.

"Since we have been given only three days to complete our preparations for the operation, the following principles will guide our planning, training, and organization. The difference between what emerges in front of our eyes, inviting our rationalization, and our institutional paradigm touches on many issues, including organization, doctrine, moral values, forms of function, and so on. Realizing we are amid a transitional phase, I would like to highlight some critical issues

that can promote our learning as a military institution, and feed our reflections during the operation and in the future. Unlike our idealistic tradition that perceived war in binary terms, this campaign is going to be a very long one, and end, in the far future, in a kind of new equilibrium rather than in decisive results. If we do not change our current discourse on intelligence, we are bound to fail. Our rivals, or enemies as they are being referred to, are not just ontological objects for action. Operationally speaking, they are a logical medium for systemic deliberation, and unless we construct them as conceptual artifacts, we deprive ourselves of the basic conditions for designing our own logic. Moreover, no intelligence apparatus is capable of providing us, prior to operations against a subversive rival, with precise and relevant information. Therefore, we need to explore the implicit rather than explicit variables, and complement the production of intelligence, or our learning about the rival, in the course of the operation through the application of maneuvers. Finally, we must attune our institutional learning to comply with the dialectics of unique contexts, of singular patterns, in the same manner that we have done here today."

"We will apply a fractal maneuver swarming simultaneously from every direction and through various dimensions on the enclave of Balata. We will completely isolate the camp, in daylight, creating the impression of a forthcoming systematic siege operation. Our policy rejects the use of tanks and artillery; machine gun fire is only allowed in conditions providing a clear field of fire, precise fire, and targets that are detached from buildings. Remember, due to the poor quality of construction, the buildings cannot sustain even low-caliber single shots. I assign the western sector to Yoni who will command Nimrod (reconnaissance), Udi (parachute anti-tank company), and Guy (parachute sappers); the northern sector goes to David; the eastern sector I assign to Roni; and the southern sector to Amir. Remember, we are not in a hurry. This operation is not about ideal modes of decision (winning). We have to avoid casualties among civilians at all cost and kill or capture the combatants, while avoiding casualties in our own units. Once we have crossed the littoral, each unit (company-sized combat team) reflects in its mode of action both the logic and form of the general maneuver—this is what fractals are all about. According to the logic implied by this new form of maneuver, each unit will combine three components in its operation—observation teams, sniper teams, and teams that are supposed to attract the attention of the insurgent fighters. Our movement through the buildings will push them into the streets and alleys, where we will hunt them down. By doing that, we will smooth the intrinsic striation of the enclave."

David, Aviv's alter ego and the most senior of the unit commanders, exploited a respite in Aviv's brief and popped in: "What is crystallizing here is exciting, yet extremely challenging in terms of execution. I would like to illuminate some practical aspects concerning the relations between cognition and maneuver in the context of the current operation. The prevailing maneuver paradigm is about geometrical order, physical cohesion, and massed firepower. Its conceptual coherence is embodied in its formal simplicity. Moreover, since similar patterns of space are being utilized by the competing symmetric contenders, the rationale of emerging operations is deterministic and the problem of self-orientation, both geographically and cognitively, by individual tactical commanders is a minor challenge. Once we shift from modes of action based on presence to modes of action based on disappearance, and from a maneuver framework reflecting Euclidean geometry to a maneuver framework reflecting the geometry of complexity, we magnify the space for exploiting our potential, yet at the same time we push the cognitive challenges for warfighters to new extremes. Since every unit commander is an autarkic fractal component within an emerging fractal system, the cognitive problem of self-orientation becomes three-fold. First, at every moment of the evolving operation the unit commander has to refer his relative position to the geography. Second, at every moment of the evolving operation he has to refer his relative position to sister units functioning within the relevant operational space. And, third, at every moment of the evolving operation he has to draw the systemic implications from his positioning in relation to the logic of the emerging maneuver as a whole. The first is about navigation, the second is about orientation, and the third is about systemic awareness. I mean awareness not in the sense of recent American clichés but rather in the sense of a cognitive quality implying synthesis. Therefore, we need to prepare navigation aids, to invest in developing common spaces of understanding in the fighting units, and to design a command architecture enabling dynamic learning in action."

A wide smile spread across Aviv's pleasant face. "One last issue before we depart. We know where exactly lies the allegiance of the Palestinian refugees living in what has become an enclave. Yet, remember they are victims not only of our wrath but also of the sympathy of the insurgents who exploit them. In other words, a most deadly game in which they are the ultimate victims in every sense has been imposed on them. Be careful! Show respect! And, pay attention to their pragmatic needs!"

"Any questions or remarks at this point?" asked Aviv. "Well, there is a lot of work ahead of us…"

With these final remarks, the war council dispersed.

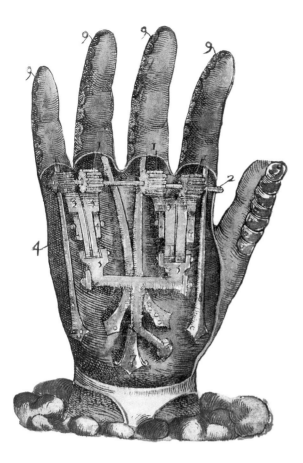

NOT A HAPPY FRACTION OF A MAN
GABY WOOD

In the mid-sixteenth century, the great French surgeon Ambroise Paré discovered what he described as a "strange and grievous fact." As surgeon to François I, Paré had accompanied the king on military campaigns of exceptional brutality. Thousands of French cavalrymen were killed and wounded by arquebuses, precursors of the musket that looked like small hand-held cannons and could blast even the most heavily armored bodies to pieces. Paré treated the wounds made by these weapons with turpentine and rose water, and he pioneered a safer method of amputation. But while creating his signature tourniquets, he found he could not tie up arteries without bruising nerves as well. The "strange and grievous fact" that arose as a consequence was that men who had lost their limbs felt the limbs to be still there. Not only did the patients imagine them, but they sometimes felt pain in these limbs, tried to walk on their non-existent legs, or reach for objects with a missing arm. Paré designed artificial body parts for his amputees, beautiful constructions to be made in metal by armorers, but he could do nothing for these strange configurations of the mind.

Paré was the first to set down the phenomenon in writing; centuries later, in the course of another war, the writer and neurologist Silas Weir Mitchell gave it a name. He said his patients were suffering from "phantom

limbs"—since these "vivid hallucinations" were in fact a form of haunting. "Nearly every man who loses a limb," Mitchell wrote, "carries about with him a constant or inconstant phantom of the missing member, a sensory ghost of that much of himself."

Mitchell was thirty-three years old when he became a contract surgeon for the Union Army during the American Civil War, a conflict that saw unprecedented numbers of men made limbless. His arrival at Gettysburg just after the famous battle made a deep impression on him, and ensured that he would despise war to the end of his days. There were 27,000 wounded to be cared for when he got there. Mitchell said he "smelt nine hundred smells," and later spoke of "the dead Confederates … with arms and legs in rigid extension—a most horrible memory." Walt Whitman, who spent the war working in a field hospital as a volunteer nurse, described seeing the remains of countless surgeries. There was, he wrote, "a heap of feet, legs, arms and human fragments, a full load for a one-horse cart."

But amputation was safer and less painful than it had been before—ether and chloroform were now used, and the longer operating time these allowed made for more effective stumps. Mitchell was eventually placed in charge of Turner's Lane Hospital in Philadelphia, which received a large number of nervous cases, and he made his reputation on the research he conducted there into nerve injuries and gunshot wounds. He identified the condition that was to become known as "shell shock," but was occupied more specifically with the thousands of amputees who populated the Philadelphia "Stump Hospital."

Writing in a popular magazine in 1871, Mitchell estimated that about 15,000 men across the country had lost an arm or a leg during the war, though only 6,075 of them had been supplied with artificial limbs so far. (In fact, there were around twice that many amputations conducted in the Union Army alone. And in 1862, a year after the start of the war, the American government officially began providing funding for one free prosthesis per amputation for soldiers and sailors.) The sheer number of patients Mitchell saw allowed him to observe the "strange and startling phenomena" associated with phantom limbs, a form of neuralgia he concluded must stem from inflamed or otherwise damaged nerves in the amputee's stump. Far from being an unusual condition, it was one Mitchell found to be present in all but five percent of cases, and he could offer no explanation for the exceptions. He saw one man who was so sure of his missing arm that he went riding and used the lost hand to grasp the reins, causing an accident. Another thought he had punched someone, but realized he had taken aim with his phantom fist. A third complained of chronic nausea, since every time he sat down to eat he tried to pick up a fork and felt sick at his failure.

"There is something almost tragical, something ghastly," Mitchell wrote, "in the notion of these thousands

above: Artificial hand, from Ambroise Paré's *Instrumenta chyrurgiae et icones anathomicae* (Surgical Instruments and Anatomical Illustrations), Paris, 1564.

of spirit limbs haunting as many good soldiers." Indeed, in many cases he found a curious version of the commonly held belief about ghosts—that people who have died violently are condemned to roam the earth in the condition in which they have been left. Some amputees in Mitchell's care found their phantom limbs stuck in the position in which they had last felt them; the last real sensation in the limb remained forever, so that a phantom hand might be paralyzed with the thumb cutting into the palm, or the fingers rigid in agony.

In the course of his article, Mitchell mentioned another, which had been published anonymously years earlier in the *Atlantic Monthly*. It was a "humorous sketch," a "*jeu d'esprit*," he said, whose fictional protagonist—a man who had lost all his limbs during the Civil War—was so realistically drawn that a number of readers had erroneously sent donations to him at the Stump Hospital. Mitchell portrayed this earlier article as an irresponsible piece of writing, and claimed that his own would describe, correctly and scientifically, the experiences of those haunted by phantom limbs.

As it happens, however, Mitchell was only correcting himself. "The Case of George Dedlow," as the *Atlantic Monthly* article was called, was Mitchell's first attempt at writing fiction—a second career in which he was to excel. Far from being funny, it was a portrait of a man who had lost everything, including his sense of self, and it clearly succeeded in eliciting a good deal of sympathy from a general public who had until then believed, along with most doctors, that phantom limbs were all in the mind.

In the story, Dedlow describes himself as "not a happy fraction of a man." His arms are blown off, and later in the war he loses both legs: "Against all chances I recovered, to find myself a useless torso." He still feels his missing legs, however, and explains the medical reasons for this in layman's terms: the nerve, which once led to the extremity and remains in the stump, "is like a bell-wire. You may pull it at any part of its course, and thus ring the bell as well as if you pulled at the end of the wire."

Gradually, Dedlow experiences a psychic loss more dramatic than the physical loss of his limbs; as he lies in hospital, motionless and bed-bound, he feels his identity beginning to erode. He wonders "how much a man might lose and yet live," since "to lose any part must lessen his sense of his own existence." Dedlow is so bewildered by his loss of self that he feels "like asking someone constantly if I were really George Dedlow or not. ... At times the conviction of my want of being myself was overwhelming and most painful."

The story ends with a visit Dedlow makes to a spirit medium, who summons his amputated legs from the afterlife. They identify themselves—rapping on the table—by two numbers: their catalogue codes from the United States Army Medical Museum. Dedlow is, he says, "reindividualized," returned to himself, and so entranced by this spirit communication that he walks across the room on invisible legs, astonishing everyone with his miraculous behavior, before sinking feebly to the floor.

Mitchell's short story was an exaggeration, of course, but it encapsulated a number of things connected with phantom limbs, and by extension, with the artificial limbs designed to replace them. The limbs are called phantoms because they are felt manifestations of something that does not physically exist—they are, in Mitchell's words, "sensory hallucinations." But they are also phantoms in their connection to the spirit world—produced, like the ghosts of the dead, in response to a loss. No matter what the neurological explanation for the phenomenon, phantom limbs are a form of mourning—the body's, or the mind's, way of making up for what has gone. Whenever surgeons performed repeated amputations, shortening the stump incrementally in an attempt to rid the sufferer of his delusion, the phantom would return with a vengeance, reasserting itself with every loss. So much is the phantom limb connected to the notion of an afterlife that Lord Nelson, on losing his right arm in battle, believed the phantom arm that replaced it to be "direct evidence for the existence of the soul." If an arm could survive amputation, he proclaimed, why should an entire person not live on after death?

In a book called *The Phantom Limb Phenomenon* (1978), Douglas B. Price and Neil J. Twombly collected a number of accounts, from the tenth century onwards, of the miraculous restoration of lost body parts, a common folkloric trope that they argue is related to the experience of phantom limbs. After all, is a person who believes his lost limb to have been restored to him by a miracle so different from the person who, sometimes weeks or years after the wound has healed, becomes conscious of his missing limb? Mitchell reported one case in which a patient had no phantom limb at all until two years after the amputation, when a mild electrical current was passed through his body, at which point he grasped at thin air and shouted in pain: "Oh, the hand! The hand!" "No resurrection of the dead, no answer of a summoned spirit, could have been more startling," Mitchell wrote. Might the religious and medical narratives be analogous?

One of the miracle tales, so famous as to have been painted repeatedly (in one depiction by Fra Angelico) concerns a leg transplant performed by two saints, Cosmas and Damian. Summoned by Pope Felix to help a man whose leg is cancerous, Cosmas and Damian cut off the man's leg. But "where," they ask, "shall we get flesh to fill up this void?" The angel Raphael appears to them and tells them that an Ethiopian has just been buried in a graveyard nearby. They are to dig up his body and cut off his leg. Then, the angel instructs them, on the day of the resurrection, they must orchestrate a swap. The saints do as they have been told, and sure enough, once the exchange has been effected, they see that each leg has become attached, by some miracle, to the person by whom they had lain it. The dead Moor

has one white leg, and the man who had cancer awakes to find his leg fully functioning, though it is clearly, by its color, someone else's.

"Putting then a candle nearby," reads one account of this awakening, "when he saw nothing wrong in the leg, he thought that he was not who he was, but someone else." Another account, a poem printed by William Caxton in 1483, reads as follows: "and when the seke man a woke/ and felte no payne/ he put forthe his honde/ and felte his legge with-oute hurte/ And thenne tooke a Candel/ and sawe wel that it was not his thye/ but that hit was a nother/ And when he was wel come to hym self/ he sprange oute of his bedde for joye."

This story is not unlike that of George Dedlow needing to be reminded, as his physical self becomes more alien to him, that he is who he thinks he is. But unlike George Dedlow, this man does not recognize himself because he has acquired a body part that is foreign to him—something new has been added. In that respect, he is more like a patient described by the contemporary neurologist Oliver Sacks. "The man who fell out of bed," as Sacks calls him, suffers from a delusion that is a reversal of a phantom limb: he thinks his own leg is someone else's, stolen from the dissecting room and placed under the sheets of his hospital bed as a joke. But when he tries to throw the leg out of the bed the rest of his body goes with it, since it is in fact his own, and still attached. He ends up on the floor, and can't get up, because the leg he sees is so seemingly separate as to be of no use to him. He can't make it move because he is so disgusted by it that he is unable to accept it. He is horri-fied by the leg, calls it "ghastly," "uncanny," "a counterfeit," and expresses some astonishment at the idea that anyone should have gone to such lengths as to manufacture "a facsimile."

In the story of the saintly transplant, it is no accident that the leg donor is a "Moor." The transplant is considered a miracle because the impossible has been performed: the donor was initially dead (so some form of resurrection is involved), and the knitting together of nerves, muscles and tissues required is so complex that surgeons are only now, in the twenty-first century, beginning to achieve success with such grafting of limbs. But part of the shock, for the patient and his acquaintances, is that the new, function-ing body part should be so completely foreign to the white man. When he starts to walk around, no one who sees him believes the miracle until they go to the graveyard and see for themselves that the dead Ethiopian now possesses a white leg, that there has been a straight swap.

To the original readers of this story, there could be nothing more foreign to white skin than black skin. Taken metaphorically rather than literally, the scene is about one's sense of identity—not about limbs at all, but about a state of mind, about the splintering of the self. In the Caxton poem, the man has to wait a while before he is "wel come to hym self": before he is fully awake perhaps, before he has "well come" to his senses. But also, before he is welcome; like

"the man who fell out of bed," he cannot rise until

he accepts who he is.

How many owners of artificial limbs have felt some-thing like this when their prostheses were first delivered? How alien must they feel to themselves? What happens to phantom limbs when they are usurped by wooden or metal pretenders to their position? While researching these issues, Oliver Sacks came across an interesting fact. Far from get-ting in the way of an artificial limb, a phantom limb turns out to be a prerequisite for wearing one. "All amputees," Sacks wrote in his book *The Man Who Mistook His Wife for a Hat*, "and all who work with them, know that a phantom limb is essential if an artificial limb is to be used." A fellow neurolo-gist had written to Sacks that the phantom's "value to the amputee is enormous. I am quite certain that no amputee with an artificial lower limb can walk on it satisfactorily until the body-image, in other words the phantom, is incorpo-rated into it." "Thus," Sacks concluded, "the disappearance of a phantom may be disastrous, and its recovery, its reani-mation, a matter of urgency. This may be effected in all sorts of ways. … One such patient, under my care, describes how he must 'wake up' his phantom in the mornings: first he flexes the thigh-stump towards him, and then he slaps it sharply—'like a baby's bottom'—several times. On the fifth or sixth slap the phantom suddenly shoots forth, rekindled, *fulgurated*, by the peripheral stimulus. Only then can he put on his prosthesis and walk."

Another of Sacks's patients described the way in which his prosthetic limb helped with the pain in his phantom. "There's this thing," he said, "this ghost-foot, which some-times hurts like hell—and the toes curl up, or go into spasm. This is worst at night, or with the prosthesis off, or when I'm not doing anything. It goes away when I strap the prosthesis on and walk. I still feel the leg then, vividly, but it's a good phantom, different—it animates the prosthesis, and allows me to walk."

The phantom, in other words, atrophies and causes pain without the prosthesis to give it purpose, and the prosthesis can only function when animated—literally given a soul, as Nelson would have it—by the phantom. The limb-wearer becomes a man-machine, given bionic life when "fulgu-rated" or "faradised," like the monster in Mary Shelley's *Frankenstein*.

The most recent research into phantom limbs, con-ducted by the American neurologist V. S. Ramachandran and popularized in his book *Phantoms in the Brain*, shows that the phenomenon may be connected to a sort of "arti-ficial man" in the human brain. There is, on the brain's surface, a map of the body in the awkward shape of a man. The map is known as "the Penfield homunculus." In the homunculus, the hand and thumb are next to the face. When Ramachandran experimented with a phantom hand patient by lightly rubbing his cheek, the patient confirmed that he felt the rubbing in his missing hand. In other words, in cases of phantom limbs, the brain receives messages in a neighboring area, though that area is not, on the exter-nal human body, adjacent. Other patients confirmed this theory. For example, two people reported sensations in their phantom foot when they had sex, and were astonished to discover an explanation for this: in the brain, on the Penfield map, the genitals and the feet are next to each other. "I never suspected," Ramachandran wryly concludes, "that I would begin seeking an explanation for phantom limbs and end up explaining foot fetishes as well."

But Ramachandran also wanted to help his patients who had pain in their phantoms, or found them paralyzed, as Mitchell's patients had, in the position in which they'd last felt them. He developed a novel technique for this, which involved giving the patient the impression that the phantom they felt but could not see was physically present. He constructed a "virtual reality box," with a vertical mirror inside it and two holes in the front. He asked patients to put both arms through the holes and to move them about in tandem. With the mirror apparently reversing their arms, the patients saw their phantoms actually move. In some cases the paralysis ended; in others the phantoms disappeared altogether, along with the pain. What appeared to have been performed, as Ramachandran put it, was "the first example in medical history of a successful 'amputation' of a phantom limb." "Philip," he said of one of his patients, "seemed to think I was some kind of magician" and indeed the "virtual reality box" he invented is not unlike the cabinet tricks used by stage magicians in the nineteenth century. The doctor had cured a delusion using illusionism.

This article is published as part of *Cabinet*'s contribution to *documenta 12 magazines*, a collective worldwide editorial project linking over seventy print and on-line periodicals, as well as other media. See <www.documenta.de> for more information on documenta 12 and this project.

below: Case of Corporal David D. Cole, New York Cavalry, presented in *Photographs of Surgical Cases and Specimens* by George A. Otis, M.D. The eight-volume series, comprising photographs of Civil War injuries, was published 1865–1881 and circulated mainly to doctors and medical colleges. Cole was wounded as a twenty-three year old at the battle at Amelia Court House, Virginia, on 7 April 1865 by a musket ball that passed through his left leg. Amputation was performed on 1 August 1865 and the stump healed favorably. On 22 November 1865, he was sent to Dr. E. D. Hudson in New York for an artificial limb fitting. By 1868, he was walking without a cane.
overleaf left: *Swimming Lesson No. 5*, 2004.
overleaf right: *Swimming Lesson No. 2*, 2004. Photos courtesy Herrmann & Wagner Gallery.

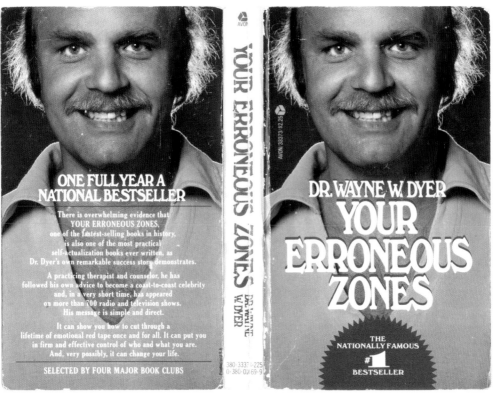

1977 Avon paperback cover with author photograph by Henri Dauman.

1979 Avon paperback cover with author photograph by Henri Dauman.

UNWELL
BRIAN DILLON

*Variable, and therfore miserable condition of Man; this min-
ute I was well, and am ill, this minute. I am surpriz'd with a
sodaine change, and alteration to worse, and can impute it to
no cause, nor call it by any name.*

    —John Donne, *Devotions upon Emergent Occasions*

TORMENTED HOPE

Hypochondria is an ancient name for a malady that is always
new, capricious, and unpredictable. Of course, the hypochondriac himself (he is traditionally male) fears precisely
the novelty of any alteration whatever in his physical being,
and conceives of health as an unlikely state in which nothing
happens to the body at all. In this ideal condition of stasis,
the skin is a perfect and inviolable envelope, the heart attains
a regularity that renders its rhythm imperceptible, and the
other organs are taxed only to the extent that they should
not atrophy, but function serenely, without labor. In reality, this is, literally, no way to live. Ideally, hypochondriacs
would like to feel nothing; but they are beset by confused
signals. Theoretically, the hypochondriac might present to a
physician with any one (or any combination of) an endless
array of symptoms gleaned from direct experience, panicked
recourse to a medical dictionary or the Internet, or a vague
penumbra of skewed fact and secondhand suspicion. In
practice, hypochondriacs often arrive at their doctors' surgeries with remarkably similar ailments. Often, the head and
neck are affected; the patient is dizzy; he is distracted by the
sound or sensation of his own pulse; he has a persistent and
inexplicable cough. He suffers from indigestion, is wracked
by abdominal pain, or distressed by irregularities of the
bowel. He has palpitations, high blood pressure, a propen-
sity to sigh or to get out of breath. His back hurts, his skin
itches or stings, he is convinced of his own unpleasant body
odor. Bizarrely, his symptoms affect mostly the left side of
the body.

    None of this would have surprised a seventeenth-
century physician. Nor, as he concluded that his patient
was suffering from hypochondria, would he have meant to
imply that these ailments were entirely imaginary. Histori-
cally, hypochondria is first of all a physical disease, with a
distinct, if often unruly, symptomatology. For the Greeks, the
hypochondrium was the region of the abdomen just below
the rib cage; Hippocrates and Celcus describe the area and
its potential disorders. Plato, in the *Timaeus*, identifies this
part of the body as the seat of both physical and exigent
emotional urges: "That part of the soul which desires meats
and drinks and the other things of which it has need by
reason of the bodily nature, they placed between the midriff
and the boundary of the navel ... and there they bound it like
a wild animal which was chained up with man." This inti-
macy between abdominal disorder and emotional upheaval
prevails until the time of Robert Burton, whose *Anatomy of
Melancholy* (1621) essays the first modern description of the scope of hypochondriacal affliction.

Burton adduces a species of *hypochondriacal melancholy*,
the definition of which already suggests the contemporary
meaning of hypochondria: "Some are afraid that they shall
have every fearful disease they see others have, hear of, or
read and dare not therefore hear or read of any such subject." Like melancholia, hypochondria here starts to lose
its connection to an earlier, humoral, model of the body's
economy, and begins to be understood in terms of a more
general character or temperament. The hypochondriac
becomes a personality type, a stock figure whose comic
potential—his suggestibility, his enthrallment to quack doctors and apothecaries—is exploited in Molière's *Le Malade
imaginaire* (1673).

THE ENGLISH MALADY

In 1685, Thomas Willis writes: "Though it has been vulgarly
held that the affects called hypochondriacal are caused for
the most part by Vapours arising from the spleen, and running hither and thither; yet in truth these distempers are
for the greatest part convulsions of the nervous parts." The
hypochondriac suffers "failings of the spirits, a danger of
swooning ... fluctuations of thoughts, inconstancy of mind,
a disturbed fancy, a dread and suspicion of everything."
Nerves account, for the next three centuries, for much of the
physical and psychic suffering that cannot be ascribed to
other, more visible or tangible, factors. The nervous type is
understood actually to suffer, but to have a hand too in the
production of his own symptoms. This nervous component
is responsible also for the image of the hypochondriac as
especially sensitive, both bodily and spiritually. He literally feels things others cannot. In *A Treatise of the Spleen
and Vapours: or, Hypochondriacal and Hysterical Affections*
(1725), Sir Richard Blackmore, physician to William III and
Queen Anne, notes that the general public is apt, however,
to mistake this sensitivity for madness, to make of the hypochondriac "an Object of Derision and Contempt."

    Sir George Cheyne, in his influential study *The English
Malady* (1733), suggests a more practical understanding
of a disorder that seems endemic to his own nation. Fully
one third of "people of condition" are said to suffer from
hypochondria at any one time: a result, he says, of their
very wealth and luxury. Hypochondria is occasioned by
"the Moisture of our Air, the Variableness of our Weather
... the Richness and Heaviness of our Food, the Wealth
and Abundance of the Inhabitants ... the Inactivity and
sedentary Occupations of the better Sort ... and the Humor
of living in great, populous and consequently unhealthy
Towns." The two most prominent British hypochondriacs
of the century—Samuel Johnson and James Boswell—
seem to have agreed with Cheyne (though Johnson
deprecated his conclusion that hypochondria and genius
went together too). Boswell wrote of his friend's hypochondria: "all his labors and all his enjoyments were but
temporary interruptions of its baleful influence," while
Johnson counseled his biographer to refrain from drunken-
ness and sexual excess, lest "horrid ideas" should take
hold of his weakened mind.

Le Malade imaginaire.

Imp. Mourlot Frès

classe des citoyens ... la providence ... sont divins, le bienfait ... que
pharmacie ... Car

a place from which he could re-imagine the world he was leaving behind. The first step in this progressive detachment from life was his habit of sleeping during the day and socializing, and later working, during the night. He shut out sound, light, and air, dosed himself with opium, caffeine, and barbital ("you're putting your foot on the brakes and the accelerator at the same time," admonished a friend) until, bedridden, all he could do was write.

SUSPENDED IN DARKNESS

Given the history outlined above, and especially in the light of the links between hypochondria and such similar but distinct maladies as hysteria and melancholia, one would think that Sigmund Freud would have had something direct and substantial to say on the subject. In fact, Freud's deployments of the term itself are ambiguous: it is as if the diagnosis of "hypochondria" relied on a counter-model to his own developing terminology. "The position of hypochondriasis," he writes in 1909, "is still suspended in darkness." Elsewhere, however, he makes cursory references to an origin in sexual trauma or excessive masturbation, and defines the condition vaguely as "the state of being in love with one's own illness." It is perhaps due to Freud's evasiveness on the subject that the diagnosis of hypochondria vanishes for much of the twentieth century, while the type—unofficially labelled as crock, incurable, or malingerer—certainly does not.

centuries, several types of physical and spiritual feebleness compose a sort of hierarchy of sensitivity to one's surroundings. The poetic imagination is famously conceived by Wordsworth as a form of passivity: a state in which past feelings and impressions (chiefly of the natural world) are to be transformed by memory. But there is a continuum of less rarefied sorts of susceptibility. Among women, a particular "sensibility" is to be cultivated towards nature—its first paradox, of course, is that this organic affinity, like all "natural" tastes, has to be worked on, rationally perfected—but it can easily revert to its morbid antipode: hysteria. In other words, a degree of oversensitivity, even of hypochondriacal illness, is considered a cultural good, but too much will simply short-circuit the relationship between irrationalism and feminine attractiveness, resulting in insanity.

This madness, in the Romantic period, is called hysteria; its (generally) masculine equivalent is hypochondria. (The novels of Jane Austen are important in this regard, but so too are the alienated, oversensitive characters of Hans Christian Anderson, himself a miserable hypochondriac.) In a sense, all of Romantic literature and art is intensely hypochondriac: unable to establish a solid boundary between the self and the world, given to guilt-ridden self-medication (as in the cases of Coleridge and De Quincey), or obsessed by the details of impending death (Keats). The most dramatic hypochondriacs, however, are not the poets of high Romanticism, but those who came later, whose constitutions seem to have been marked by the sickly fears of their predecessors and increasingly alarmed by the scientific discoveries of their contemporaries. Alfred Lord

Tennyson is a particularly poignant example: a poet who seems to have thought that his visionary calling literally involved *seeing things*. He became debilitatingly obsessed by the floaters that hovered before his eyes: "these 'animals' ... are very distressing," he wrote. His particular fantasy of bodily invasion shows the idea of infection stealthily invading the imagination of the nineteenth-century hypochondriac.

But perhaps the most rigorous observer of the relationship between real illness and the mind's invented ailments is Charlotte Brontë. She seems to have experienced two dramatic bouts of hypochondria. The first overcame her at a lonely boarding school on Dewsbury Moor: "I endured it but a year, and assuredly I can never forget the concentrated anguish of certain insufferable moments, and the heavy gloom of many long hours, besides the preternatural horrors which seemed to clothe existence and nature and which made life a continual waking nightmare." She suffered the second in Brussels in 1843, when she was left alone during the summer holiday at the school where she was working. Brontë dramatizes this second crisis in *Villette*: her heroine Lucy Snowe descends into a fog of melancholy and obsession when she is left alone during the summer vacation. Having recovered from her own uprising of hypochondriacal passion, she recognizes it instantly in another's face, glimpsed at the theater: "Those eyes had looked on the visits of a certain ghost—had long waited the comings and goings of that strangest spectre, Hypochondria ... dark as Doom, pale as Malady, and well nigh strong as Death. ... And she freezes the blood in his heart, and beclouds the light in his eye." Brontë's own sufferings in this regard might plausibly be said to have their origin in the scenes of sickness and death that she witnessed in the family home at Haworth; an early encounter with illness or bereavement has long been posited as one of the triggers of adult hypochondria. But Brontë also means something else by her self-diagnosis: a certain sensitivity that is bound up, in Romantic fashion, with her status as an aspiring writer.

ON THE EXPRESSION OF EMOTIONS

In 1812, Benjamin Rush wrote that a diagnosis of hypochondria was generally "offensive to patients": it had acquired the sense of an imaginary illness, a state of malingering or delusion. By the end of the century, it seems established as a psychological illness, still retaining a wide array of symptoms and possible causes. George Savage wrote in 1892: "The word *hypochondriasis* has a very wide meaning, and includes forms of insanity, as well as many disorders which cannot properly be so called. Under this name we shall have to describe a nervous disorder varying from slight oversensitiveness to insanity with marked delusions and actively suicidal tendencies." Gradually, the patient's reported physical sensations have been written out of the actual description of the disease: they have become ghost symptoms, mere feints executed by the actual, underlying illness.

opposite and overleaf: illustrations by Honoré Daumier for an edition of Molière's *Le Malade imaginaire*, ca. 1850.

Le malade imaginaire.

Je suis perdu.... il faut faire mon testament.... ils vont m'ensevelir.... m'enterrer.....
adieu !

Imp. Mourlot Frès

SEARCHING FOR SEBALD:
PHOTOGRAPHY AFTER W.G. SEBALD
THE INSTITUTE FOR CULTURAL INQUIRY

Paperback, 8 x 10 inches
450 pages / 120 color and 350 b&w
$39.95 ISBN 1-889917-11-7

W.G. Sebald's unique use of images in his hybrid writings is the starting point in this engrossing study. In addition to 400 images, 17 theoretical essays consider Sebald through the filters of art history, film studies, cultural theory, psychoanalysis and photographic history and theory. Includes a rare , previously unpublished interview with Sebald.

ANNETTE MESSAGER:
WORD FOR WORD: TEXTS,
WRITINGS AND INTERVIEWS
LES PRESSES DU RÉEL/D.A.P.

Hardcover, 7.75 x 10.25 inches
416 pages / 280 color and 20 b&w
$65 ISBN 1-933045-35-3

The most comprehensive survey to date on French artist Annette Messager, best known for her conceptually playful work dealing with words and langauge. Includes many works from the 1970s through today, numerous texts from the course of her career, interviews, and Messager's own notes and reflections.

B-ZONE: BECOMING EUROPE
AND BEYOND
ACTAR/KUNST-WERKE BERLIN

Paperback, 6.25 x 7.75 inches
416 pages / 300 color
$40 ISBN 84-96540-05-7

B-Zone is a collaborative research and art project that investigates ongoing changes to the social and political geographies of the Balkans. The three core projects that make up the book each follow the trajectory of a large-scale piece of infrastructure laid down in a former Communist state, treating the sites and lands as palimpsests.

OLIVER PAYNE & NICK RELPH
JRP/RINGIER

Flexibound with carpet, 6 x 8.5 inches
196 pages / 120 color
$38 ISBN 3-905701-45-6

Oliver Payne & Nick Relph's new book is jacketed in the durable, stain resistant fabric of London Underground seat upholstery and rings like a cell phone when it is opened. Inside, it contains the first print transcripts of the artists films, including Driftwood, Gentlemen, Comma, Pregnant Pause, *and* Sonic the Warhol. *A crowd of authors addresses topics that have inspired the duo in their work.*

SOVIET TEXTILES:
DESIGNING THE MODERN UTOPIA
MFA PUBLICATIONS

Paperback, 8 x 9 inches
96 pages / 52 color
$24.95 ISBN 0-87846-703-3

Between 1927 and 1933, as the new Soviet Union emerged and the Communist party struggled to industrialize the state, a group of young artists pitched in by designing fabrics depicting tractors, smokestacks and symbols of collective modernity, cloth with which to mold its buyers into ideal Soviet citizens. 40 prime examples of these rarely-seen textiles are gathered in this publication.

PINK: THE EXPOSED COLOR IN
CONTEMPORARY ART
AND CULTURE
HATJE CANTZ PUBLISHERS

Hardcover, 6.75 x 9.5 inches
283 pages / 200 color
$45 ISBN 3-7757-1771-4

Few colors trigger more contradictory associations and emotions—tender, childish, plastic, pornographic—or are so symbolic of both high and low culture, which is exactly why pink makes for such an interesting study. Artists of all hues are included in this unusual intercultural discourse, from Jean-Honoré Fragonard to Pipilotti Rist.

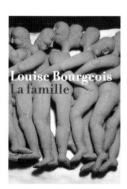

LOUISE BOURGEOIS: LA FAMILLE
VERLAG DER BUCHHANDLUNG WALTHER
KÖNIG, KÖLN/D.A.P.

Hardcover, 7 x 9.5 inches
242 pages / 150 color and 20 b&w
$45 ISBN 3-86560-075-1

Louise Bourgeois has long placed the psychology of family at the center of her work. This thematic gathering of works, made between 1935 and 2005 in a broad range of media, is by virtue of the centrality of family to the artist's oeuvre, an overarching retrospective, a focused view of her career.

9 EVENINGS RECONSIDERED:
ART, THEATER, AND ENGINEERING,
1966
MIT LIST VISUAL ARTS CENTER

Paperback, 8.25 x 13 inches
88 pages / 4 color and 60 duotones
$25 ISBN 0-938437-69-0

In 1966, a Bell Laboratories physicist brought a group of avant garde artists together with 10 openminded members of the science and technology fields for 9 Evenings. The happenings, documented here, counted John Cage, Yvonne Rainer, Robert Rauschenberg, Oyvind Fahlstrom and others among the participants.

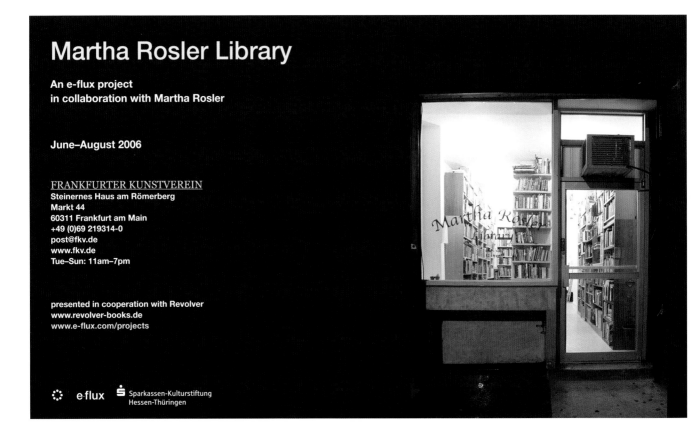

Sutapa Biswas
Birdsong

Douglas F. Cooley Memorial Art Gallery
Reed College, Portland, Oregon
August 29—October 8, 2006
web.reed.edu/gallery

In conjunction with the Portland Institute for Contemporary
Art (PICA) 2006 Time-Based Art Festival / www.pica.org

Birdsong is an Institute of International Visual Arts (inIVA) touring exhibition produced in collaboration with Film and Video Umbrella. Supported by Arts Council England, AHRB, Chelsea College of Art and Design (University of the Arts, London), The Culture Company, Magnesium Elektron and the University of Southampton. A specially produced monograph on Sutapa Biswas is published by inIVA in collaboration with the Douglas F. Cooley Memorial Art Gallery, Reed College, Portland, Oregon with contributions by Ian Baucom, Guy Brett, Sutapa Biswas, Laura Mulvey, Moira Roth, Griselda Pollock and Stephanie Snyder.

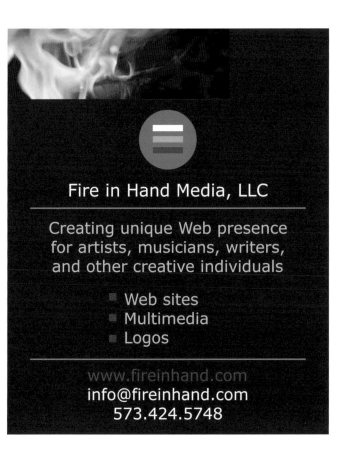

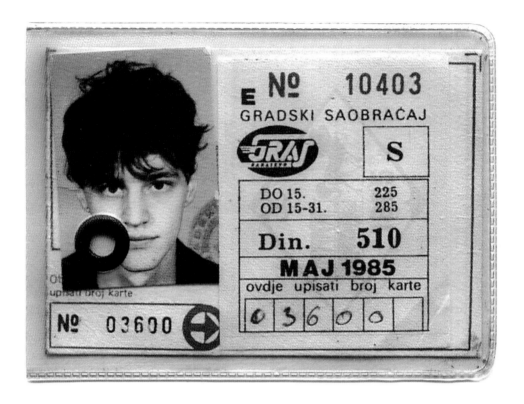

BALKANISATOR

info@defunktcentury.co.uk

C A B I N E T B P Q E
D D R U W V K Q Z L M
Q U W P H F V B W I J
U O O K L Q Y H I V L
R A S W Y C L B S E F
E T N H U F V B H L D
M L Z Q F X D C H O N
O L V W O I H G I Y K
E S G N V R T R X N L
G Q D W Y X A O D N S
O I S V M R P F O U C
P J J L T H Z I E R I
W D V T R T B T P X Q
A B M C X D G K E R Y
F V R A O B V P L I C
M Q O N S R K M N L O
C Z N G A L U E A P K
R P V L H B T U X D S
T N X E C C S S R O L
G H Z I X Q G B V H N

CHEAP   RECTANGLE   EYEBALLS
HALF PAGE   FULL PAGE   QUARTER PAGE
ADVERTISING   GOOD VALUE   FOUR COLOR
CABINET   IMPRESSIVE   501C3
NONPROFIT   IMPACTFUL   SAVVY
BROOKLYN   SUCCESS   SUBLIMINAL

cabinet word search

CABINET BACK ISSUES

Available back issues (pictured here) are $10 each + shipping.
Shipping rates: US $2 per issue; Can & Mex $7 for 1, 2, or 3 issues; Eur, Au, & NZ $9 for 1, 2, or 3 issues.

Note: tax-deductible donations of $250 or more will be thanked with a sold-out issue (2, 3, 4, 5, 6, 7, 8, 9, 10, 11, 14, 16, 18, or 19) of the donor's choice. Supplies limited.

Issue 1
**Invented
Languages**

Issue 12
The Enemy

Issue 13
Futures

Issue 15
The Average

Issue 17
Laughter

Issue 20
Ruins

Issue 21
Electricity

CABINET UNLIMITED EDITIONS

Priced postpaid to US destinations
For international rates, email orders@cabinetmagazine.org

Weather Mugs and Glasses
by Bigert & Bergström
(from Issue 3, *Weather*)
$15 each

Glow-in-the-dark Evil/Exit vinyl sign
by Vincent Mazeau
(from Issue 5, *Evil*)
$25

A view of Mount Rushmore in 500,000 years
poster by Matthew Buckingham
(from Issue 7, *Failure*)
$15 — ships rolled

Acumulus Nobilitatus
poster by Paul Noble
(from Issue 10, *Property*)
$15 — ships rolled

Alphabetized Newspaper
poster by Rutherford Chang
(from Issue 15, *The Average*)
$15 — ships rolled

New World Order giftwrap
by 2x4
(from Issue 16, *The Sea*)
3 sheets for $10 — ships rolled
On the actual giftwrap, the animals are silver

CABINET 2006 LIMITED EDITIONS

Priced postpaid to US destinations
For international rates, email orders@cabinetmagazine.org

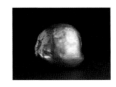
C Note, 2005
by Jude Tallichet
Hand-engraved aluminum sculpture
Edition of 100; signed and numbered; 6 x 5 x 5 inches
Courtesy of the artist and Sara Meltzer Gallery
$500 (editions 1–50) $600 (editions 51–100)

Mill Creek Valley, 2005
by Matthew Buckingham
Digital C-print
Edition of 100; signed and numbered; 18.5 x 25.5 inches
Courtesy of the artist and Murray Guy Gallery
$500

CABINET BOOKS

Special postpaid price to US & international destinations
Subscribers: Take an additional $5 off the listed price.

Odd Lots: Revisiting Gordon Matta-Clark's Fake Estates
On artist Gordon Matta-Clark's *Reality Properties: Fake Estates*
$27 (US); $35 (Can & Mex); $45 (Elsewhere)

Letters from Mayhem
Illustrations by Roger Andersson, text by Albert Mobilio.
$27 (US); $35 (Can & Mex); $45 (Elsewhere)

The Paper Sculpture Book
Do-It-Yourself paper sculptures by 29 artists
$27 (US); $35 (Can & Mex); $45 (Elsewhere)

HOW TO ORDER

1 Mail a check to "Cabinet" 55 Washington St #327 Brooklyn NY 11201
2 Shop online at www.cabinetmagazine.org/shop
3 Fax Cabinet at +1 718 222 3700.
4 Call Cabinet at +1 718 222 8434.

Checks must be in US dollars and drawn on a US bank.
Cabinet accepts Visa, MC, AmEx, and Discover. The website also accepts PayPal.